SPECTACULAR
VERNACULAR

To our fathers,
who showed us the harmony
of integrity and adventure.

House in Djenné, Mali.

Book design by Scott Knudsen.

Printed in Japan.

Library of Congress Cataloging in Publication Data
Bourgeois, Jean-Louis, 1940-
    Spectacular vernacular.

    Bibliography: p.
    Includes index.
1. Architecture—Arid regions. 2. Vernacular architecture.
I. Pelos, Carollee, 1939-
NA2542.A73B68   1983   720'.915'4   83-479
ISBN 0-87905-144-2

SPECTACULAR VERNACULAR
A NEW APPRECIATION OF
TRADITIONAL DESERT ARCHITECTURE

Text by
Jean-Louis Bourgeois
Photographs by
Carollee Pelos

➜P

Gibbs M. Smith, Inc.
Peregrine Smith Books
Salt Lake City
1983

TABLE OF CONTENTS

Preface ix

The Image of the Desert 1

Water, Sand, and Snow 5

Mud Stands Up: Construction Techniques 7

Mud In Our Eyes 13

Walls and Roofs 17

Wind and Ventilation 53

Sacred Mud: Sahelian Mosques 69

Asking the Good and Strong: Afghan Muslim Shrines 87

David and Goliath: Mud vs. Money 89

Notes 93

Photographic Notes 99

Bibliography 101

Acknowledgements 105

Index 107

PREFACE

A *traveler must have a falcon's eye, an ass's ears, an ape's face, a merchant's words, a camel's back, a hog's mouth, and a stag's legs.*

English proverb

This book is a celebration. It documents, discusses, and defends mud vernacular architecture of the desert. Briefly, vernacular is local, folk, or popular building. The term stands in contrast to the traditions of high-style, formal monuments designed to display the power and taste of a ruler or elite.

We began as veterans of the New York "viz biz," or visual business—Carollee a photographer, Jean-Louis an art historian and critic. Inspired by published photographs of lovely vernacular buildings, we became convinced that, somewhere out there, gleamed many more gems unknown to foreigners. In October 1978, we two neophyte vagabonds boarded a bus in Istanbul and began to meander towards Delhi.

In Iran we were primed and eager to study the ingenious windtower. We found our first pair under a gorgeous rainbow (nature can be so maudlin). But they proved to be our last. History, in the form of a persistent Ayatollah, actually had the gall to interrupt our research. We fled to Afghanistan.

It was in that wonderful country, while being tossed out of a sensitive region, that we got our first big break. We had told the local army commander what was perfectly true—that we were looking for working horizontal windmills (figs. 47, 48). But the commander was a reasonable man, and it was clear that such a preposterous story from Americans prowling near the Iranian border was proof that we were either liars or crazy.

He "invited" us to accompany his courier on a twenty-hour jeep trip out of his area and his hair. We "thanked" him. And it was from a jammed, damned jeep that we first saw, rising from the flat desert like a

mirage, the most gently surreal, breathtaking building we've seen before or since (see plate 52). Our faith was confirmed. Beauty *does* lie in the "next" village. Or the next. Or next. No matter. It's there.

We gathered material in Mauritania, Senegal, Mali, Niger, Morocco, Iran, Pakistan, Afghanistan, and India. Our two trips, in 1978-79 and 1980-81, totaled twenty-one months. We logged about 15,000 miles by shoe, canoe, ox and horse cart, tractor, bus, and, mostly, truck. Hired jeeps would have isolated us. The informality of local transportation enabled us to meet people whose knowledge, good-will, and hospitality often proved crucial in remote areas.

We ate local food, drank local water, and were never ill. Our most remarkable nutritional incident was bizarre but harmless. Deep in the desert in northwest India, after days of nothing but rice, we wolfed a luscious mess of mutton. At this sudden influx of protein, our bodies signaled ''Oh boy!'' with an *Alice In Wonderland* sensation. We thought we were growing. For twenty wierd, glorious minutes we both felt eight feet tall.

Desert heat can be intense. But because the air is dry, the heat is rarely as agonizing as a muggy August scorcher in Manhattan. Heat sizzled us out of only one town. We were later consoled to learn that one inhabitant—the story goes—having died and gone to Hell, is spending eternity wrapped in blankets, shivering.

During days of woe, when the beauty hid and the road stretched endless and our eighty-pound packs turned to solid lead, we invoked our basic rule: rabid despair was permitted, but only one of us was allowed to grovel in it at a time.

Traditional people are deeply, movingly hospitable. Over and over they were wonderful to us. We tried not to take advantage. One way we sought to return the warmth we met so often was to take and mail back more than a thousand individual and group photographs.

Given this book's subject, where, some may wonder, are buildings from Yemen, Morocco's High Atlas, Algeria's M'zab, or Mali's Dogon? The answer is that generally we chose to stalk the little known or unknown. The immediate problem is that many superb, remote examples are disappearing month by month. Vernacular architecture, however, is not quaint, to be preserved merely because outsiders may like it. It is a vital expression of an autonomy which deserves to survive—and *shall* survive, we believe—and prosper.

A wise person has said, ''Traveling in the company of those we love is home in motion.'' We are pleased that, soon, we again will be home in the Sahara.

Jean-Louis Bourgeois
Carollee Pelos
New York, March 1983

THE IMAGE OF THE DESERT

Fig. 1

The desert. To those of us who live in temperate zones, the word has associations both appealing and sinister. We picture a landscape unobstructed, totally visible and visitable; we feel secure because no person or thing can approach unseen. Like the sea, the desert can feel refreshingly vast, its surface uncluttered by ground cover, its space spared the illegible busyness of a complex middle distance. Place seems very open, clean, and basic.

But the desert can as easily assault as refresh. Its heat and glare can be brutal. Its openness may be read as a lack of spatial definition which starves eye and soul. Ironically, total physical clarity can become perceptual obscurity. Both "here" and "there" often fade into anonymity— into somewhere, then anywhere, then nowhere. A stranger to its cues, the mind unfamiliar with its subleties identifies the desert with sensory deprivation. But as Saint-Exupéry, one of its great poets, has observed, "If the desert is at first only emptiness and silence, it is because it does not offer itself to one-day lovers."[1]

Fig. 2

Foreign sensibilities tend to picture the desert not only as a physical landscape but as a moral one. In contrast to its imaginary complement, the jungle, whose principle seems to be excess, fertility run riot, the desert is perceived as a place of absence, of essential simplicity—a setting of either voluntary self-denial and high purpose or involuntary deprivation and despair.

Only two types, we generally suppose, can inhabit such a landscape: the heroic and the hapless. The first includes the "explorer," the missionary, the soldier, the anthropologist, the development technician—all conveniently Western. The second, those without choice, are those "condemned" to live there. Afraid of the unfamiliar, we call the desert "empty," just as we call Africa "dark," unaware that the ignorance these terms point to is ours.

Deep in our picture of the desert lies that symbol of mystery, Timbuctoo. The city hovers in our mind's eye half unknown fact, half fantasy. The strange syllables do indeed name a real place, an ancient trading city on the southern edge of the Sahara where the mighty Niger River loops north. But seen on a map or visited, Timbuctoo remains legendary, a vision of remoteness and inaccessibility as fabulous as El Dorado, Atlantis, or Xanadu.[2]

Aside from its actual past, Timbuctoo has a history as myth. True, the city was once a starting point for caravans carrying gold north across the Sahara.[3] The city was rich. But hearsay inflated these facts into fable, the glorious fiction of a city whose roofs were covered in gold.[4] Since Timbuctoo long remained unvisited by Europeans, variations of the vision thrived.[5] In the 1820s Tennyson mused:

...[M]ethought I saw
A wilderness of spires, and chrystal pile
Of rampart upon rampart, dome on dome,
Illimitable range of battlement
On battlement, and the imperial height
Of canopy o'ercanopied.[6]

The myth of Timbuctoo included architecture monumental and majestic.

This version of the legend suddenly collapsed. In 1828 a young French explorer, René Caillié, was the first European to reach Timbuctoo and survive. His account deflated the splendor.[7] Timbuctoo's wealth had vanished. Tennyson describes the disappointment:

[Y]on brilliant towers...
Darken, and shrink and shiver into huts,
Black specks amid a waste of dreary sand,
Low-built, mud-wall'd, barbarian settlements.
How chang'd from [that] fair city![8]

Still, the magic endures. As phantom capital of the exotic desert, veiled in innumerable dunes and a dash of danger, Timbuctoo remains in mental maps around the world the symbol of "far away." A new myth has emerged, no longer imperial, but pastoral. Once an image of exotic sophistication, Timbuctoo still haunts the Western imagination. It has become the epitome of the desert settlement, insulated by distance from industrialization and hence in tune with a landscape harsh but—more crucially— unspoiled.

Again, myth and reality diverge. In contrast to its profoundly rural image, Timbuctoo has for some years been an important administrative center possessing its own airport. Ten days by camel to the west, virtually unknown and extremely isolated, Oualata (plates 3, 10, 12-19), actually is what renowned Timbuctoo is imagined to be. The settlements are ancient rivals. Both cities were for centuries caravan ports. From them, camels bearing gold powder, slaves, and pilgrims bound for Mecca began the grueling journey north to Morocco, returning with salt as well as cloth, rugs, and other Arab and European goods. Oualata was probably founded in the seventh century, some four hundred years before Timbuctoo, and became a major trade center after 1200. In the fourteenth century, it appeared on European maps and for two hundred years outshone Timbuctoo as a commercial, religious, and intellectual center. Later, Timbuctoo surpassed and eventually eclipsed it.[9]

Timbuctoo's legend has long outlived its splendor. Though still a universal symbol of mystery, the city itself has largely disappointed travelers for over 150 years. Tiny and obscure, Oualata again triumphs over her famous rival. The riches she boasts are only made of lime on mud. But they are dazzling.

A great belt of desert stretches, with breaks, halfway around the world. Starting in China, it passes west through India, Pakistan, and Afghanistan, continues through the Near East, crosses Africa as the Sahara, and, leaping the Atlantic, ends in Mexico and the southwestern United States.

Contrary to its popular image, the desert has many faces. Only ¹/₆ of it consists of dunes. A great deal is gravel, boulder, or salt, a great deal mountainous (plates 1-4). Much of it flowers, often profusely, during an annual rainy season which varies upward of a few weeks. Vegetation—or lack of it—shifts by almost imperceptible degrees from areas like Niger's "desert in the desert" (where the area's single tree was a famous landmark), through many variations to savannah, where small and widely spaced thorn trees dramatize an intense but tolerable dryness (figs. 1 and 2).

The architecture of the desert also shows tremendous variety. Nomads have developed tents of extraordinary lightness and durability. Palaces of stone and mosques of fired brick and tile rank among the world's great monuments. Between fabric and pole on the one hand and chisel and kiln on the other lies that most forgiving of materials, sun-dried mud, a constituent of the shelter, in varying climates, of some 1.5 billion people.[10]

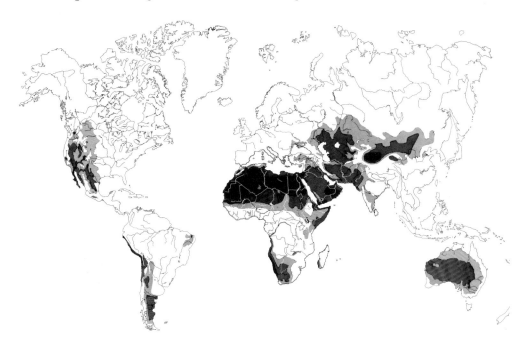

ATER, SAND, AND SNOW

Water governs the position of architecture above, on, or in its site. Depending on how much water is present, a building may hover, sit, or burrow. At the aqueous extreme, stilts suspend the house over a lake or stream. At intermediate stages, the building insulates itself against ground damp with water-resistant materials. Toward the arid extreme, structure and site are so compatible they begin to blend.

The arid extreme includes the Arctic. Ice and snow may chemically be water, but physically they are not. An arctic snowbank is as dry as a dune. The igloo is much like a mud building in the driest desert. Since both must insulate occupants against temperature extremes, both are thermal fortresses, with massive walls and minimal openings.[1] Where Mother Nature's breath freezes and sears, she compensates. Her flesh, soft and abundant, is easily formed into thermally-sheltering cocoons. Both igloo and mud dwelling are in total harmony with a waterless site. Built of its local "soil," each is an artificial cave.

In many deserts, stone is rare and wood too scarce to fuel brick kilns. As a result, traditional desert architecture is largely built of sun-dried mud. By temperate climate standards, mud is disconcertingly, even alarmingly soft, a substance so fragile that, when hearing of its use as a building material, many people scoff. How, after all, can one build serious structures presumedly no more rugged than that symbol of the ephemeral, a child's sandcastle on the beach?

Such skepticism brings to mind a story. Over fifty years ago, a group of African sheiks, desert dwellers traveling outside the Sahara for the first time, were taken to see a large waterfall. They were astonished. For a long time they stared, mesmerized. When finally their guide suggested there were other sights to visit, the group explained that they were waiting. "For what?" asked the guide. "For the water," said the sheiks, "to stop."[2]

Secure in our familiarity with our own climate, we may—with either empathy or malice—smile at the sheiks' innocence. But imagine the tables turned. Imagine the feelings of a Westerner first glimpsing the Great Mosque of Djenné in Mali (plates 27-30)—the shock, the disbelief, the awe at such monumentality in such a perishable material, mud. Our innocence is a mirror image of the sheiks'.[3]

In temperate zones, only children or the playful build with pure mud or snow. True, even in the relatively humid climate of England, France, and Germany, mud is a serious building material when properly compacted, alloyed, armatured, or shielded.[4] And a popular saying in the southwest of England reminds us that a mud wall will last for centuries if kept dry with "a good hat and a good pair of shoes," that is a broad eave against rain and a sound footing against ground damp.[5] Without hat, skeleton, shoes or other improvement, however, building with mud in temperate zones is child's play. The material is pliable and responsive but vulnerable. The sandcastle, like the snowman, is the very symbol of fantasy and fragility, powder masquerading at permanence, softness at solidity.

But in the desert, mud is dependable, the stuff of sanctuary as well as play. If, as the philosopher Gaston Bachelard says, "the house protects the dreamer,"[6] then desert building, offering itself as both the shelter and the subject of dreams, reaches the primordial poles of our imagination: it forms images of both security and energy, both peace and expression.

Among vernacular architectures, that of the desert is a special case. Despite many obvious differences, desert architecture resembles that of temperate climates in an important way—buildings must protect occupants from seasonal and daily heat and cold. In the humid tropics such protection would be inappropriate. There, unmodified ventilation provides comfort, not distress. Shelter from nature is needed from above, from sun and rain, but not from the side. Buildings are basically umbrellas, not envelopes as in arid and temperate zones.

Temperate and desert attitudes toward the wall are compatible in some ways, incompatible in others. In both cases, the wall has a physical as well as a social function. It is substantial, not merely a screen. Consequently, people from temperate climates read the desert dwelling as providing a psychological security absent in a vernacular building in the humid tropics, whose open form and woven materials connote "temporary camp" rather than "home." Desert vernacular is, in this regard, more familiar, more vicariously accessible as a place of permanent comfort not just for "them," but for "us."

On the other hand, Westerners may read as unwelcoming or claustrophobic that desert windows are small and rare. We reason from the wrong sky.[7] Microscopic, reflective dust particles suspended in the air compound the sun's brilliance into an acid light. Massive mud walls turn the house into a thermal, optical, and psychological fortress. Windowless buildings are friendly—refreshing islands of cool dimness in an ocean of heat, glare, and often stinging dust (plate 4).

MUD STANDS UP: CONSTRUCTION TECHNIQUES

It is rare in the desert or savannah to find an isolated dwelling. Traditional houses tend to cluster. The fields, where farmers grow such grains as millet and wheat, and the grazing ranges for herders' camels, goats, or cattle lie outside the settlement. In villages and some cities, households tend to live in extended-family compounds, with separate sleeping, kitchen, and leisure structures facing a common open area. In towns and other cities, a courtyard house may share windowless walls with its neighbor.[1] Generally, dwellings turn inward (fig. 3).

In traditional desert architecture, buildings tend to be designed, built, decorated, and maintained by ordinary people—men, women, and children—not full-time specialists. In some areas, it is true, master masons plan and supervise the erection of major structures such as mosques.[2] But even where trained builders work constructing a house, the entire family works too, often with relatives and neighbors. Generally, the men are

Pl. 5

Pl. 5. Making mud bricks with a double mold.

PL. 8

Pl. 8. Applying mud relief.

responsible for raising walls and roof, the women for finishing interior surfaces (plates 5, 8, 10).

A single rainy season, though mild, will soften a mud structure's finer detail. Untended after several such seasons, a mud building may begin to "melt." But mud architecture in the desert may last an extremely long time provided it enjoys regular, minimal maintenance. This maintenance consists largely of replastering. Women or men, depending on the culture, keep the house's exterior in good repair. Acknowledging rather than defying time, upkeep is as cyclical as the harvest. It is a dry season activity during which swirling hands, applying new mud like balm on weathered skin, heal the erosion of annual rains (plate 11). Some architecture in mud is now more than four hundred years old.

Desert architecture is the product of a relatively simple yet highly effective technology.[3] Sand and clay are dug from the ground and mixed with water and, usually, chopped straw. The sand is an inert filler; the clay provides cohesion; the straw, by helping the mass to dry evenly, minimizes cracking. Local recipes vary widely depending on the soils available and may include organic materials such as sap, animal milk, blood, or dung.[4]

There are three general methods of building in mud. In some areas, the mixture is tamped in place using a large wooden form, or *coffer*. The block is allowed to dry, the coffer is removed and lifted on top of it, and the process is repeated. This is *pisé*, or *rammed earth*, construction[5] (plate 7).

A second method, used in northern Sudan, is called *coursing* or *puddling*.[6] A thin layer of mud is shaped by hand. After it dries, another is added, and the wall rises. Indians in the southwestern United States customarily used coursing until the seventeenth century, when the Spanish introduced the cast, sun-dried brick.[7]

Brick is the third technique. Dating from before recorded history,[8] it is the method in widest use today. Sometimes, hand molded bricks dry in the wall; more frequently, cast ones are left on the ground to bake in the sun (plates 5, 6). Set in place, the bricks are usually joined by mud mortar and covered with mud plaster. This technique is called *adobe*, a word borrowed from Spanish. Still earlier, Spanish borrowed it from Arabic, in which *al-tob* is the type of earth from which sun-dried bricks are made.[9]

One of mud's great advantages is thermal. Usually up to two feet thick, mud walls have a high heat-retaining capacity. During the day, acting as passive-solar collectors, they insulate well against high temperatures, and at night the heat they have absorbed is slowly released. While outside temperatures may soar or fall dramatically, indoor ones stay remarkably constant.

Pl. 1

Pl. 1-4. Ranging from high mountains to low-lying plains, the desert is characterized by extreme heat and cold, intense glare, and, often, stinging dust.

Pl. 3

Pl. 6

Pl. 7

Pl. 2

Pl. 6. Mud bricks drying in the sun.

Pl. 7. The ''rammed earth'' or pisé technique.

Pl. 4. A mild sandstorm.

Pl. 10. After a wall is plastered, decoration may be applied.
Standing on a stack of beds, a woman incises a pattern.

Pl. 11. After the rainy season, the wall is often replastered.

MUD IN OUR EYES

Vernacular desert architecture is ''new.'' True, the tradition of building in sun-dried mud is older than recorded history. But the tradition for the first time is prompting a growing interest among ''foreigners.'' People in the temperate-climate, industrialized world are finding aesthetic, practical, and theoretical value in the traditional architecture of the desert.[1]

Important parallels and contrasts mark the histories of Western interest in primitive art and vernacular architecture.[2] Around 1904, artists such as Matisse and Picasso were struck by the expressive power of African sculpture beyond tribal function.[3] In art, the primitive and the modern were not antithetical; rather, the opposite. They were immediate allies, both at war with an academic naturalism perceived as superficial and decadent. But if one of the ethical and aesthetic hallmarks of modernism was ''purity,'' primitive art qualified and primitive architecture didn't.

Pl. 9

Pl. 9. These mud granaries are built in coils, an application on a large scale of a pottery-making technique.

The first was perceived as elemental, the second as sentimental.[4]

One strain of architectural modernism, its antitraditionalism, militates against architecture in mud. "Traditional materials in general," declared architecture critic Henry–Russell Hitchcock in 1929, "imply the past rather than the present and must be avoided."[5] Modernism's skeletal steel, and the thinness and tautness of glass, technologically and "morally" rebuke mud's earthy mass.

Today, the machine is no longer an unquestioned cultural icon.[6] A reaction has begun. Interest in the broad spectrum of vernacular springs in part from the current de-mythologizing of progress and technology.[7] In the earlier appreciation of primitive art, the "natural" was an aesthetic norm and was attacked; now it is a moral ideal and vigorously defended. In architecture specifically, disillusionment with Modernism's glorification of the individual "heroic" architect[8] and a growing demand for climate-responsive and user-responsive building has led to a profound questioning of the purpose and means of architecture. Enthusiasm for vernacular is today's version of a theme recurrent in architectural history—the search beneath the conventions of the moment for the original, the simple, the essential.[9] Our own standards of chastity having changed, vernacular is now celebrated as a touchstone of purity: architecture in practical, spiritual harmony with its site and society.

In the history of the study of vernacular architecture, Bernard Rudofsky was a pioneer. His 1964 exhibition and subsequent book *Architecture Without Architects*[10] were significant—and controversial. His wide-ranging collection of photographs introduced a new theme to a broad public: the beauty of non-industrial, non-Western, and—as he put it—"non-pedigreed" architecture. The response was overwhelming. The exhibition, "Architecture Without Architects," was shown in eighty-four museums and galleries around the world.[11] The book was translated into five languages, remains in print, and to date has sold over a hundred thousand copies, an astonishing figure for a volume on such an esoteric subject.

Rudofsky inaugurated a new way of seeing. Until then vernacular had been regarded as mere ethnographic information. He insisted it was art. The originality of his vision was epitomized in the work's laconic, provocative title. Single-handedly challenging the established canons of both architectural history and anthropology, he trusted the enthusiasm of his own taste and, by feisty fiat, elevated a broad spectrum of building from shelter to architecture.[12]

Since the 1960s, the artist in our society has achieved new prestige. Once, alienated and alienating, the avant-garde artist assumed the moral stature to criticize a "retarded and unseeing dominant class."[13] Now many architects assign this role to a foreign exotic, the vernacular builder. Architects and writers who criticize our built environment as hyper-industrialized, ecologically unsound, and inhumane have turned to the ideal of indigenous communities as arcadias deemed "natural" because they are non-industrial.[14]

In its busy and brutal complexity, modern life is widely perceived as inauthentic. "The authentic work of art," says Lionel Trilling, "instructs us in our inauthenticity and adjures us to overcome it."[15] The vernacular settlement is now called upon to do this. During the history of Western architecture, various types of free-standing, so-called "primitive huts" were ideals of authenticity. But now that environmental design has supplemented or subsumed the building of single structures, the new, more global discipline needs a paragon of clustering, of community. It half discovers, half projects what might be termed an ideal "aggregate 'primitive hut,'" at once sophisticated and natural—the vernacular settlement.

Early aesthetic enthusiasm for primitive art isolated it from the societies which produced it. But the exhilarating idea, to adapt Rudofsky's phrase, of art without artists, was denounced by anthropologists as irresponsible and ethnocentric. This disapproval paralleled the cool academic response to the visual emphasis in Rudofsky's work.[16] *Architecture Without Architects* includes little written commentary.

Imagine a Western "pilgrim" who seeks and finds, deep in the desert, an isolated, undocumented vernacular settlement. Suppose the architecture strikes a responsive chord in the visitor, that it is beautiful—perceived as some transculturally accessible blend of grace, intelligence, or power. It is an exciting moment. The cultural prospector has discovered a nugget, perhaps a mine, and out come the tools of cultural acquisition—camera, tape-measure, compass, and notebook. In a particular patch of architectural arcadia, our pilgrim will spend from an hour to two weeks. Often, local conditions are favorable and a stay's length is freely chosen. If so, its duration depends on the architecture's quantity and perceived quality, and the coincidence of skills—sometimes absent—in a common language to learn about construction, age, use, and symbolism. The pilgrim then moves on.

Back home, the pilgrim's built environment consists largely of solids once molten, now cool and rigid. Plastic, asphalt, glass, modern cement, and steel are congealed ex-soups. Part or all of each has been heated to hundreds, even thousands of degrees. In the production of building materials, the hotter the process, the visually and psychologically colder—more alienating—the product. But since the heat of the sun is by comparison mild, sun-baked mud looks and "feels" soft. Not cooked out of the natural cycle, it is a product less of powerful, mechanical ingenuity than of the earth, molded by hand.

The joy—or bias—this book celebrates is delight in the human touch in architecture. By and large, both contemporary public sculpture and modern architecture have tended to celebrate the virtues of industrial alloys—their strength, precision, grandeur, durability. These are traditionally masculine qualities. The direct molding and carving of form, the expression of feeling and of meaning—traditionally artistic activities—are largely absent from sculpture and architecture today. Since the art we need is rare at home, we seek it abroad. And since throughout the world, technology is breaking nourishing links to place and past, the pilgrim is eager to document as fast as possible buildings which celebrate a threatened vitality.

Much of the "truth" of architecture is not visual. And it is obvious that—even if blessed with that sweet miracle, the intelligent, patient, and articulate informant—a couple of weeks in a village is, in terms of learning about a culture, an instant. Such a brief visit can garner only hints of an architecture's deepest local meanings: how design, social space, and symbol embody cultural concerns.[17]

Back home, the pilgrim's photographs are subject to Susan Sontag's warning:

"[P]hotography makes us feel that the world is more available than it really is. The knowledge gained through still photographs will always be some kind of sentimentalism, whether cynical or humanist.

"[T]he truths that can be rendered in a dissociated moment, however significant or decisive, have a very narrow relation to the needs of understanding. . . . Only that which narrates can make us understand. . . ."[18]

Largely deprived of narrative, what are we left with? Are the "alien" feelings which are stirred by objects and buildings that move us valueless or worse? Anthropologists tend to say yes.[19] Faced with forms and symbols whose local meanings escape us, we are enjoined to be silent, with the occasional hint—discreet because the subject is explosive—that formal, foreign analysis of the work would imply narcissistic neglect of the culture and, at bottom, racism.[20]

A key current feature of the aesthetic appreciation of vernacular is the absence of discussion. This critical silence is not a simple omission. Well-intentioned, but oversensitive authorities on anthropology, environmental design, art history, and art criticism have, in a rare display of cooperation, agreed to preach and practice verbal abstinence. Vernacular's "beauty" is mentioned, however intensely, with little or no analysis. In design circles the temptation to imitate "exotic form"— often qualified as "mere"—is frequently cautioned against.[21]

Until now, vernacular architecture has usually been either simply displayed, with only cursory analysis, or studied as "expressive"—as cultural geography— with emphasis on its relation to local society and setting, investigators perceiving themselves as objective. Opposed to both approaches—unexamined formalism and self-suppressing empathy—is Oscar Wilde's opinion that "[T]he highest Criticism deals with art not as expressive but as impressive purely."

"Criticism's most perfect form," suggests Wilde, "seeks to reveal its own secret and not the secret of another."[22] Criticism's "own secret" can be seen as the attitudes and motives—many unconscious—it inevitably brings to its task, and its "most perfect form" as including the search to make these explicit to itself and its audience. Such reflexive impressionism and analysis requires more self-awareness than does the role of the "objective" observer.[23]

The acknowledgment that strategies and images of dwelling can affect the observer as deeply as the observed revives sensibility as a legitimate, even necessary, subject of discussion. Applied to vernacular it focuses the insights of cultural geography not only outward, but inward, toward the depth and complexity of the observer's own ethnic, climatic, and aesthetic attitudes and the radical way these shape architectural expectation and perception.[24] This procedure clarifies our pleasure, till now largely mute, in specific exotic form and design. Examination of outside observers' necessarily foreign, widely divergent "lenses" broadens the study of vernacular to include architectural criticism.[25] It is largely the outsider's specific innocence that makes the architecture in this book legitimately spectacular.

Fig. 3

Fig. 3. In traditional desert architecture, the wall is usually undecorated. But there are impressive exceptions. Local traditions include painted and incised patterns, low and high relief, applied and free-standing columns, and virtuoso arcades.

Pl. 12

Pl. 12. On either side of many exterior doors, slates are set into the wall. Muslims preparing to pray touch the stones to cleanse themselves ritually when water is not available.

Pl. 12-19. In eastern Mauritania, West Africa, the town of Oualata long outshone Timbuctoo, its sister caravan-port ten days by camel to the east. Today Oualata is an extremely isolated community with a population of about a thousand.

WALLS AND ROOFS

In traditional desert architecture, the exterior wall is usually undecorated. Resisting the climate's harshness and expressing the importance of family privacy, structures tend to look in, not out. Foreign travelers may find monotonous the impassive public faces of village and city walls. But invited in, visitors are often delighted by the visual exuberance of bedding, carpets, and wall-hangings.

The wall, however, is not always plain. Its decoration can assume astonishing variety. Plates 12-21 and figures 4-41 illustrate examples in a progression of walls from flat through highly sculptural.

The Painted and Incised Wall
(plates 10, 12-19)
Deep in the West African desert, the town of Oualata is small, isolated, and extremely difficult to reach. Its name means "the shore of eternity." The settlement's splendor is its bold, sumptuous decoration, which women

Pl. 14. A door opening on an interior court. The decoration here is painted on a slightly raised, incised ground.

17

apply and then annually renew after the brief rainy season. On some surfaces white lime is painted directly on the mud-plastered wall. In interior courts, a slightly raised ground is prepared for most designs; then a pattern is incised and painted. Some authorities trace visual elements to Morocco[1] and even Iraq.[2] It seems that the designs may be aids to fertility and maternity.[3]

The decoration's impact springs from the contrast between two complimentary motifs, one simple, the other complex. The first consists of broad white bands which frame many doors, windows, and flights of steps. Occurring largely at edges which interrupt the massive wall, these wide stripes help turn small openings and narrow stairs, otherwise overwhelmed, into dramatic visual events.

The second motif is the arabesque, whose intricacy is heightened by the straightforward band. First seen as brilliant forms bursting on dark-red fields, the arabesques suggest the radiance of fireworks. Studied more closely, the patterns play figure-ground games. At times the thin brown lines come forward, as if drawn on white. At times the white comes forward, often dividing into discrete, vaguely human figures, often sweeping on through as a curling, plunging, continuous path of enormous energy.

Pl. 13

The arabesques display rigorous order—they are almost symmetrical around one, frequently two, axes. Their meticulous delicacy seems almost crystalline. But an underlying informality remains. For all their immaculate precision, they often float, or crown a door or window, not quite horizontally. The patterns avoid geometry's cool perfection. They retain the immediacy and freshness of freehand drawing.

Pl. 16. Arabesques appear in many courtyards in Oualata. They may well be a symbol of fertility.

Pl. 18
Pl. 17

Pl. 18. The Prefet, or Mayor, of Oualata, with his family.

Pl. 19

The Embossed Wall

(plates 8, 20, 21; figs. 4-7)

In the Kachchh region of northwest India, the glory of many houses is the interior. Punctuated by small decorative mirrors—which also festoon the women's dresses—wall after wall, sometimes whole rooms, wear intricate ribbed reliefs of zig-zags, stars, grids, waves, rosettes. Occasionally figures appear: women balancing waterpots on their heads, someone riding a camel, someone else a horse. The most frequent image is the peacock, native to the region and a symbol of good luck. Deftness, care, and whitewash transform mud into lace. The mud virtuosos are Harijan (Untouchable) and Rabari caste women. Mud in their hands—they use no molds—has a wide range, from low benches strong enough to bear the weight of thirty heavy blankets to delicately faced shelves for brass utensils.[4]

Pl. 20, 21, figs. 4-7. In Gujarat state, India, interior walls are delicately embossed with mud tracery. The artists are women of the Harijan and Rabari castes. Using no molds, they work the mud by hand into a wide variety of forms, from benches strong enough to support thirty heavy blankets to delicately faced shelves for brass utensils.

Fig. 7

Fig. 6

Fig. 4

Fig. 5

High Relief (figs. 8-27)

A striking example of a functional wall providing visual drama occurs in the pigeon tower (figs. 8, 9), common in the area around Isfahan, Iran, for over four hundred years.[5] These massive structures, often thirty to fifty feet high and up to thirty feet in diameter,[6] provided housing for pigeons in exchange for droppings used as fertilizer. Each hole had a perch. The dung was collected at the base of the wall.

The average large tower sheltered a thousand birds and produced six thousand pounds of fertilizer a years for the surrounding melon fields and fruit trees[7]. The basic design problem was to provide the maximum number of pigeon holes possible with the minimum amount of building material. Since timber was scarce and rarely used, there were no spanning elements, such as beams, that would be under tension. Instead, because only vaults were used the entires structure was under compression[8]. At the beginning of the eighteenth century there were some three thousand pigeon towers in the Isfahan area. As late as 1939, it was possible to see nearly fifty from one place[9]. But they have long been steadily decreasing in number.

In central Mali, facades display an extra-ordinary variety of high-relief (figs. 10-27). Though most buildings are a single story, they suggest monumentality by incorporating the wall of the roof-terrace above.[10] The line where roof meets wall is

Figs. 8, 9. Iranian pigeon towers were built to collect pigeon droppings for fertilizer. Each pigeon-hole is furnished with its own perch.

rarely articulated, and this ambiguity generally allows integrity of design from ground to skyline.

Figures 10-15 show examples of what might be called the "missing brick" style. In some cases (figs. 10, 11), design elements seem abruptly "punched" through a smooth, taut surface. Carefully spaced but totally isolated, missing bricks and deep windows seem to float.

By contrast, diagonals built of bricks in series express visual weight (figs. 12, 13). Wry ambiguities occur. Are the diagonals created by bricks applied or bricks removed? Which is primary, molding or carving? On one wall (fig. 13), this uncertainty is delightfully compounded by a serrated diamond which seems to hang like a pendant from the most stressful point of a mock beam. Or is the diamond's "toe" actually touching the ground, thereby making it a graceful applied column? In other buildings, a complex, single-layered lattice of bricks seems slipped over the wall like meshwork (fig. 15).

The wall acquires still other subtleties by incorporating three-dimensional themes. Casting shadows which may keep over half the wall's area in cooling shade, what might be termed the "stepped recession" motif (figs. 16-18) introduces a number of rectilinear planes.[11] As rounded, applied columns (fig. 20) rise through a roofline, they become fully freestanding. And a short, engaged column appears in both

Fig. 11

Fig. 10

Figs. 10-15. In the "missing brick" style, bricks are omitted for visual reasons. The spaces do not actually pierce the wall.

Fig. 12

raised and recessed versions on the same facade (fig. 21).

Village buildings in Mali often show the influence of the region's architectural capital, the city of Djenné. For example, on a rural entry house (fig. 22) and a Young Men's House (fig. 23), points against the sky are grouped over a central doorway. Just below them, small thin openings alternate with rudimentary applied pillars. These features are probably borrowed from the classic Djenné house facade (fig. 26) most of whose elements still grace many Djenné buildings[12] (figs. 24-26). In the Djenné area phallic projections top many corners; on the house of a marabout, or Muslim leader, they stand in a row above a whole facade (fig. 27).

Fig. 13

Figs. 14, 15. In Malian Young Men's Houses, adolescent males live apart from their families until they marry.

Fig. 16

Figs. 16-18. The "stepped recession" motif divides a wall into a subtle composition of framed and framing surfaces. Simple elements generate a rich play of shadows.

Fig. 17

Fig. 17. A two-family house.

Fig. 18. Row-houses.

Fig. 20

Fig. 19

Figs. 19, 20. Houses display a variety of columns, arches, and finials.

Fig. 21

Fig. 21. Raised and recessed versions of the same column adorn a dwelling.

Figs. 22, 23. *A rural entry house guarding admission to a walled compound and a Young Men's House in Mali display elements of the ''Djenné style.''*

Fig. 23

Fig. 24

Figs. 24-26. Djenné has long been the architectural capital of Mali. The carefully orchestrated high relief of the Djenné style features phallic projections above the facade and multi-storied applied columns flanking the doorway. The projections are adaptations of ancestral pillars that guarded gravesites and family compounds.

Fig. 25

Fig. 26

Fig. 27

Fig. 27. The house of a marabout, or Muslim leader.

Columns and Arcades
(figs 28-41)

In this last, fully sculptural aspect of the wall, we see some of traditional desert architecture's most stunning decorative and structural effects. Some seem fanciful: a tiny colonnade (fig. 28); a twisted column wriggling from base to capital (fig. 29); a fluted shaft, double molding at each end, rising from a pot (fig. 30).

On a larger scale, five porches (figs. 31-35) play simple, elegant variations on the theme of the arch—flat, gothic, round, horseshoe, and halved. Preoccupied, a pair of small columns have eyes only for each other (fig. 31 upper-left).

Two full stories of arcades ring the lee half of a Young Men's House in Mali (fig. 36). Because such fine detail could not withstand the weathering of annual rains, the other two facades, which face the rain's quarter, are blank. Open, the lower arcades permit sociability; screened, the upper ones provide privacy and shade. Direct yet delicate, phalluses are at once powerful and decorative. Intricate, sculpted decoration has a thermal as well as a visual function. It both casts shade on a wall and provides increased surface for heat loss.[13]

Fig. 28

Fig. 28. Figure/ground games. Do we see columns or openings? Free-form teases symmetry in a charming house in Senegal.

This progression of walls climaxes with three houses' abacus-like colonnades in Senegal (figs. 37-41). In this rare and vanishing style, the most ornate elements are not applied, but weight-bearing. Though slight and apparently frail, each supports an enormous load. The contrast between visual delicacy and structural strength seems at times whimsical, at others awesome.

Fig. 30

Fig. 29

Fig. 31

Figs. 31-35. Covered arcades admit air and light yet protect families from rain and direct sun.

Fig. 32

Fig. 34

Fig. 33

Fig. 35

Fig. 36. Open and screened arcades adorn a phallus-studded Young Men's House.

Figs. 37-41. Porch arcades on three houses in Senegal. Brilliantly articulated walls show both visual elegance and structural daring.

Fig. 39

Fig. 40

Fig. 41

Figs. 42-44. In areas where there are few trees to provide long beams, interior space is spanned by many methods. In a small mosque in Niger, a set of columns supports the central lantern roof. An entry house's single central pillar is made of solid mud. And another entry house has a "Hausa dome" with saplings for ribs, a system adapted from the tents used years ago, when the Hausas were nomads.

Fig. 46

Roofs (figs. 42-46)

In areas where there are few trees to provide long beams, interior space may be spanned by a variety of methods. These range from maximum internal support (fig. 42) to none (fig. 45).

Four columns support the lantern-roof of a small mosque (fig. 42). An entry-house's single column is made of solid mud (fig. 43). Another entry-house has a "Hausa dome" which uses grouped saplings for ribs[14] (fig. 44). Ribless vaults and domes made of sun-dried brick and built without scaffolding are found throughout the Middle East[15] (figs. 45, 46).

Fig. 45

Figs. 45, 46. Ribless vaults and domes are found throughout the Middle East.

51

Fig. 47

Figs. 47, 48. Built to grind grain, an Afghan windmill with horizontally rotating sails recalls the world's earliest, invented in the region more than one thousand years ago.

W IND AND VENTILATION

Fig. 48

Desert winds vary from violent to absent. Different regions have developed highly ingenious strategies tailored to harvest or counteract local wind conditions. Devices range from those that can convert the wind's fury into power to others that shrewdly coax a cooling breeze from stifling calm.

The Horizontal Windmill
(figs. 47, 48)
The wind blows hard in western Afghanistan. Sweeping south from the Kyzyl-Kum steppes of inner Asia, a torrid gale known locally as the ''wind of 120 days'' and the ''wind that kills bulls'' howls almost daily from June through September. Often reaching one hundred miles per hour, this wind blows hardest in Sistan, a dry, hot region extending across Afghanistan's southwestern border into Iran.

Sistanis turned their meteorological scourge into a benefit. They were the first people to harness the wind, to focus the air's wild energy into work.[1] Before or during the ninth century, Sistanis invented the windmill.[2] They were perhaps inspired by horizontal, wind-driven prayer wheels which whirled in Tibet and Mongolia as recently as a hundred years ago. The sails of the first Sistani mills almost certainly rotated horizontally[3] like the millstone, thus bypassing the need for a gear to translate vertical into horizontal torque. Mills ground grain and pumped water.

Not until the twelfth century did windmills—with the familiar, vertically rotating sails—appear in Europe. And not until the late sixteenth century did they reach La Mancha in Spain. It was probably because Cervantes found their whirling sails new and strange that windmills outraged the gallant Don Quixote.[4]

Early windmills prompted not only comical pique but admiration and even wonder. Of Sistan, "the land of wind and sand," a tenth century chronicler writes, "there is no place on earth where people make more use of the wind."[5] A thirteenth century commentator even compares the Sistanis' power over the wind to that of early wind-master Solomon, the first person in legend to travel—with his entire court—on a flying carpet.[6] As late as 1963, fifty mills were still active in Neh, a town in Iranian Sistan.[7] But today working horizontal windmills have almost disappeared, superceded by mills powered by diesel motors.

In the nineteenth century, a local ruler in central Iran tried to import the horizontal windmill. At considerable expense, he built a huge mill to raise water. But the mill never pumped a quart. Local winds were far too light to turn its sails.[8] Such a mismatch of regional wind and vernacular wind-device is rare if not unique. The rule is an exquisite pairing, well shown in traditional structures using the wind, not for energy, but to cool.

To Catch a Cooling Breeze
(figs. 49-53; drawings A, B)

The strength and direction of a region's wind govern the form and size of openings designed both to receive the wind and to vent it. Near the Afghanistan-Iran border, because a powerful wind blows from a single quarter, windscoops are small[9] (fig. 46), and small ventilators are needed only over kitchens. On the other hand, Egypt's prevailing summer wind is mild, so ventilators—which help draw the breeze through a building—yawn at least as large as the quite large wind-catchers. In fact, in Egypt,[10] Algeria,[11] and northwest India,[12] free-standing porches actually face away from the wind, their back walls pierced by relatively small openings. The flow of air over and around these porches creates a low pressure within that pulls air through the openings. The reverse orientation would not allow sufficient venting to prevent the air inside from going stale.

In southern Pakistan, wind-catchers can be seen studding a distant horizon or looming over a street or roof (figs. 49-51). Depending on the light, they suggest a host of associations: periscopes, sails, huge kites, mushrooms, or elves with hats. Singly, in small groups, or as skyline legions, they have the lovely power of evoking moods like abstract sculpture.

Their design is elegantly simple. Most consist of three flat planes and a post. Two vertical surfaces at right angles form a base. A third, one of its corners tucked into the angle, tilts forward at about forty-five degrees and deflects the wind down into the house. A post anchors the deflecting plane.

Across the Sind region's flat desert, a southwest wind blows from April through June. Steady and cool, it is a blessing. Its arrival coincides with the area's most brutal heat, when the day's highest temperature averages 107 degrees F. The wind is moderate, so wind openings are large and ventilators infrequent. In a typical village hundreds of wind-catchers reach high into the sky to clear the "wind shadows" of neighboring rooflines. They turn their backs to the winter wind, which blows from the opposite quarter and is not needed indoors in cool weather.

Like that of most indigenous architecture, the history of Pakistan's wind-catchers is obscure. Local tradition states only that their use is "very old." The first Western reference to them seems to have been by an English traveler who, visiting the city of Hyderabad in 1815, observed that

Fig. 49

Figs. 49-53. Taking advantage of a cool summer wind, Sindis in southern Pakistan build wind-catchers to channel the breeze down into their houses.

Fig. 50

Fig 51

wind-catchers occurred on every house "from the governor's palace to the lowest hovel."[13]

Southwest of Hyderabad, the large town of Tatta boasts wind-catchers on most of its houses. There are interesting variants from the standard plan. Sometimes, wind-catchers do not rise from the roof but are incorporated into a building's highest story[14]. In many, the east-west axis is two or four times the north-south axis (fig. 50). In a few cases, the ratio can be as much as seven to one. Below this type extends a long, narrow "wind-room" whose entire ceiling is a wind-catcher.

An elegant, twenty-year-old house in Tatta boasts a wind-room twenty-eight feet long (figs. 52, 53; drawings A, B). On its lee wall, four windows and two doors can be opened in any combination to regulate the flow of air into two bedrooms, then through them out to an open court and its wide colonnade. In the colonnade's four walls are twenty-one doors with transoms. Eleven wind-catchers and two ventilators cool the entire house. Kitchen and toilets—and their odors—are to the lee of all bedrooms.

All wind-catchers have a metal grate to prevent entry into the house from the roof. Except for the very large ones above wind-rooms, all also have trap doors. Propping these doors at different angles governs the amount of air admitted. In winter they are shut. In multistoried houses, a shaft conveys the breeze to rooms on the lower floors.[15]

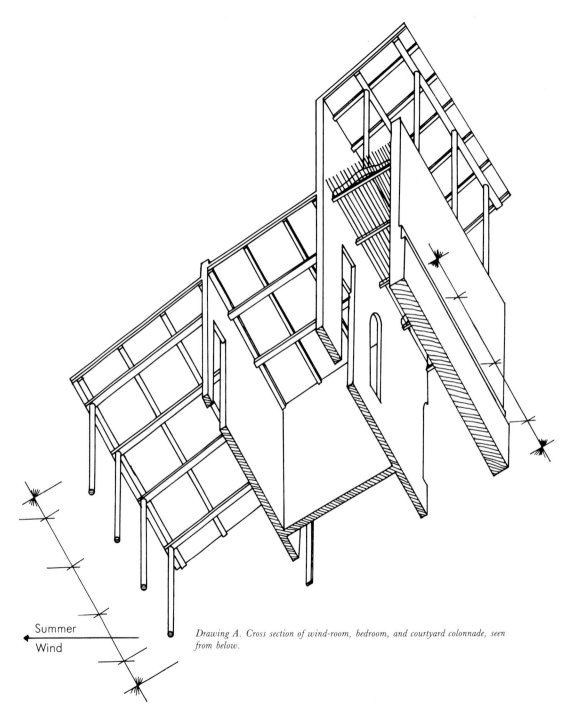

Summer Wind

Drawing A. Cross section of wind-room, bedroom, and courtyard colonnade, seen from below.

Fig. 52

Figs. 52,53, drawings A, B. A twenty-year-old house in the town of Tatta boasts a wind-catcher twenty-eight feet long. Below it, a wind-room has four windows and two doors which can be opened in any combination to regulate air flow.

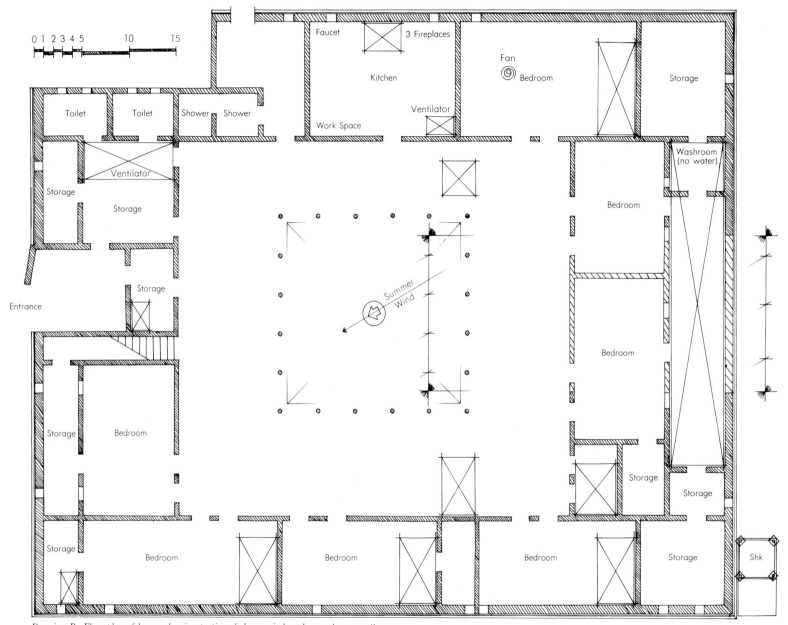

0 1 2 3 4 5   10   15

Faucet   3 Fireplaces

Kitchen

Fan
Bedroom

Storage

Toilet   Toilet   Shower   Shower

Work Space

Ventilator

Ventilator

Storage

Washroom
(no water)

Storage

Storage

Bedroom

Summer
Wind

Storage

Entrance

Bedroom

Bedroom

Bedroom

Storage

Storage

Bedroom   Bedroom   Bedroom   Storage   Shk

Storage

Drawing B. Floor plan of house, showing postion of eleven wind-catchers and two ventilators

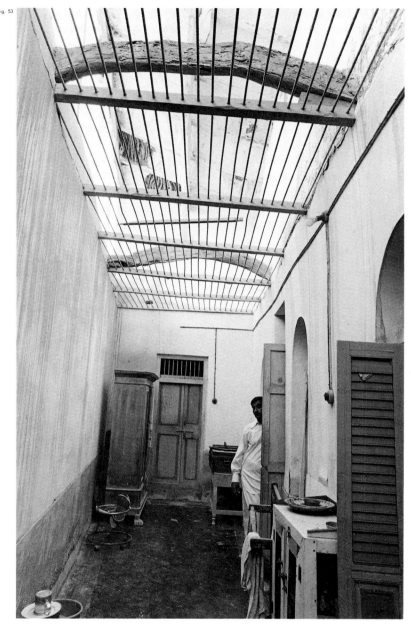

Fig. 53

Wind-catcher technology runs the gamut from traditional to industrial. In many wind-catchers, a base of sun-dried mud brick supports a deflecting plane of wood, the whole sheathed with a layer of mud mixed with dung and straw. More "modern" ones have a base of kiln-dried bricks, a plaster sheath, and a deflecting plane of corrugated steel supported by a wooden frame. The most recent ones are entirely concrete.

Though not rare, concrete wind-catchers are by no means common. They adorn virtually no recent affluent Sindi homes, whose long, low lines, it is claimed, are ruined by the wind-catcher's upright thrust. This argument skirts the real issue, which is that fashion now backs consumerism, in the form of ceiling, table, and frequently enormous free-standing electric fans. The wind-catcher, conspicuous symbol of a slower, supposedly more backward way of life, is on the wane. The rising cost of energy may soon force fashion around again.

The Stack Effect

On Iran's central plateau and along the Persian Gulf, torrid temperatures and light breezes have inspired thermal ingenuity. Wind-towers—tall to reduce the admission of dust—are topped by slender openings up to thirty-five feet high. The giant slots, connected to individual passages within the tower's shaft, function alternately as intake and outlet.[16] Facing all four quarters, they can reap the slightest, most fickle breeze. After sundown, the heat stored in the tower's mud-bricks warms the air, which—being less dense than the cooler surrounding night air—rises. This process, known as the *stack* effect, creates a draft that pulls a refreshing breeze through doorways and windows.[17]

In southern Morocco, houses tend to huddle in common defense against the sky. As in many traditional desert communities, very narrow streets hinder the penetration of hot sun and strong, dust-laden winds (fig. 54). Houses' second stories often bridge the street, creating underneath a network of cool, dark tunnels. These passages, mysterious and refreshingly humid even at harshest midday, are dimly lit by occasional light-wells called—in local translation—''God's lightbulbs'' (fig. 55, drawing C).

Maadid is a traditional, walled town of some two thousand. Like many neighboring settlements, it is built entirely of mud. Where the Iranian wind-tower employs the stack effect to cool a single

Fig. 54

Fig. 54. In many traditional desert communities, narrow streets hinder the penetration of hot sun and fierce, dust-laden winds.

Fig. 55

Figs. 55-57, drawings C, D, E. Maadid, in southern Morocco, is an extraordinary example of clustering. Second stories often bridge streets, creating a network of cool, dark tunnels underneath. These passages, refreshingly humid even at harshest midday, are aired and dimly lit by occasional open shafts locally called, ''God's light bulbs.''
One unit in a megastructure, the standard dwelling is a two-story house with a narrow front and long, common side walls. The ''stack'' effect, venting warm air out skylight and stairwell, draws cool air in from the covered street.

63

Drawing C. Cross section of typical blocks of houses

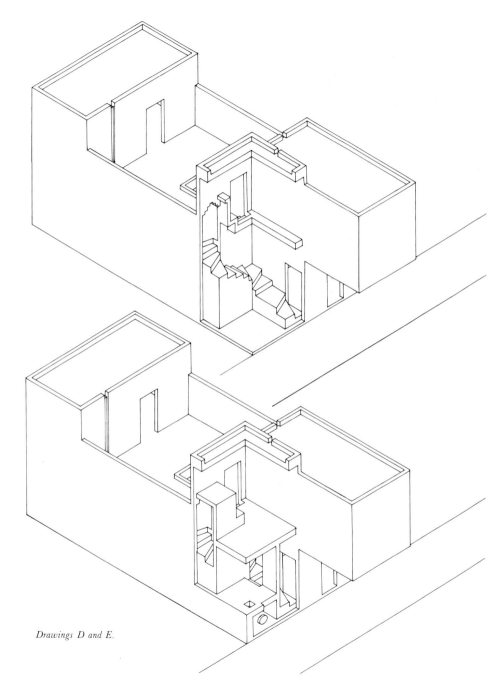

Drawings D and E.

dwelling, Maadid's design uses it to cool many. The basic unit is a two-story row house with a narrow front and long common side walls (figs. 56, 57; drawings D, E). Upon entering, one finds a small antechamber. Ahead, beyond a door and lit only by a small central skylight, is a large livingroom. At its far end stands the door to a small bedroom or storeroom. The ground floor has no external wall-windows. To one side of the antechamber, serpentine stairs turn right, then left, then right again, up past a toilet at mid-story to the second floor. Here, two rooms (or sets of rooms) face each other across a long, walled terrace.

Together, stairs and toilet are a model of functional elegance. They simultaneously allow or prohibit the passage of people, light, air, and waste. The toilet is a small opening with a date-basket lid. Below, waste is dried and deodorized by straw, collecting in a vault emptied periodically directly from the street.[18] The position of the toilet's entrance, being both at the half-story and on a stairwell which operates as a ventilation shaft, provides additional protection against odors reaching the ground floor.

As the stairs descend, the first two right angles prevent light from filtering through the toilet doorway. This is crucial because of the area's flies. Insistent, disease-carrying, and legion (particularly during the date-harvest when roofs and terraces are covered with dates drying in the sun), the flies are exasperating as well as

Fig. 57

noxious. Luckily, they are "stupid." They read dark for night, and wherever light is absent they fall asleep. Proof that design perfectly prohibits the spread of odors and the annoyance of flies is that the toilet needs, and has, no door.

The livingroom skylight provides more than light. At least as important, it allows air near the ceiling, heated by the sun striking the roof, to escape. This stack effect draws air from the covered street through the front door, habitually left open for this purpose. Cool, humid, and fresh, this sweet breeze reveals one of the street's key functions: to be the house's lung.

Maadid's superblocks of houses nestle back-to-back, flank-to-flank, and usually, above the covered street, front to front. None of the ground-floor walls have windows. And only three small openings—skylight, stairwell, and street light-well—pierce the continuous ground-floor ceiling. Finding it more convenient to burrow than to build, many traditional communities, from Spain and Tunisia through Turkey to China,[19] have carved out subterranean dwellings. Maadid's design, however, is remarkable in the degree to which it *simulates* the underground. In doing so, it acquires one of underground living's major advantages—insulation against temperature extremes—while brilliantly solving its major problem: ventilation.

Fig. 56

Evaporative Cooling (fig. 58)

Among many traditional desert devices using evaporation to cool, one is used from northern India through western Afghanistan and also in West Africa.[20] A suitable local bush is woven into a loose, thick mat or packed into a frame, placed outside a window or door, and repeatedly drenched with water. Since the process of vaporization absorbs heat, a breeze evaporating the water can easily cool a room by 15 degrees F.

In cities in India, the system is sometimes aided by a small amount of electricity. Wet mats up to eight feet tall hang before open windows to cool modern offices. Water drips from holes in the pipe from which mats hang. The run-off trickles into a pebbled trough and is recycled by an electric pump.

A more compact device, the *desert-cooler*, is about the size and shape of an air conditioner. A small electric fan draws outside air through mats of wood shavings kept damp by a pump and blows the cool air indoors. Extremely effective in dry, hot regions, the desert-cooler uses much less electricity than an air conditioner. The appliance was once popular in the southwestern United States. It deserves to be again.

Architectural devices to catch or create cooling breezes are very old. Ancient Egyptian houses featured triangular wind devices.[21] At least 1,200 years ago wind scoops caught the sea breeze on buildings in Peru.[22] As rising fuel costs make industrial air conditioning prohibitively expensive, age-old ingenuity may come to the rescue. Different meteorological areas of the world would do well to adopt appropriate wind devices—ecologically sound forms of air conditioning at once cheap, efficient, and often beautiful.[23]

Fig. 58

Fig. 58. Evaporative cooling. A traditional form of air conditioning consists of packing a local plant into a frame, placing it outside a window, and repeatedly drenching it with water. Since evaporation absorbs heat, a breeze evaporating the water can cool a room by as much as fifteen degrees.

SACRED MUD SAHELIAN MOSQUES
(plates 22-39)

Immediately south of the Sahara stretches the Sahel, a vast region with little rain, sparse vegetation, and a rich, distinctive architecture. Islam first penetrated the area in the eleventh century.[1] Three hundred years later, a Sahelian Muslim emperor, Mansa Musa, stunned the world by the amount of gold he brought with him on a pilgrimage to Mecca.[2] Through the eighteenth century, Islam in the Sahel was chiefly the religion of kings, courtiers, and merchants. Then by means of a series of regional *jihads*, or holy wars, it changed from an elite to a popular faith.[3]

As it advanced, Islam came into conflict with local animist religions. A Mauritanian account describes an ancient confrontation. In the eighth century, Yahya El Kamel, a Muslim holy man from Bagdad, was the first Arab to reach the town now known as Oualata (where a Bambara king, absent just then, had a stone of gold to which he tied his horse).

Yahya and his party asked for water. No, the Bambara replied, water was sold. But

Yahya had none of the shells then used for money. He gave his student three pebbles and instructed him to throw them down the well, one at a time. After the first pebble, the water rose to the top of the well, and the travelers drank. After the second pebble was tossed, the water sank to its original level and turned into blood. After the third, the blood turned to sand. The Bambara exclaimed "Tabre," indicating Yahya was the stronger. Yahya invited them to turn Muslim. They declined, packed their belongings, and left. The Muslims remained.[4]

The form of the Sahelian mosque is unique. Horizontal sticks stud massive towers which face east, toward Mecca. Mud-plastered walls and towers are topped by tapering, often phallic pinnacles.[5] The highest of these are frequently capped by ostrich eggs, symbols of purity and fertility.[6]

The contrast between the Sahelian and the Middle Eastern mosque is striking. In the classic mosque exquisite refinements of

mathematics, masonry, space, and tile produce airy jewels. The earth is brilliantly denied. But in the Sahel, since stone is rare and timber too scarce to fuel brick or tile kilns, construction is usually of sun-baked brick finished with mud plaster. The Sahelian mosque is closer to earth. Its color and massiveness echo hers.

Because the rainy season is short, Sahelian buildings need minimal annual repair. Maintenance is one purpose of the sticks that bristle from so many walls. The sticks form permanent ladders. They provide access to exterior surfaces for replastering The ostrich eggs have a practical use, too. Their durability (ostrich eggshells are extremely tough) protects symbolically crucial points particularly vulnerable to the rain.

In addition to their utility, sticks and eggs play important visual roles. Behind and below them, every surface and contour is molded. Though they may reach toward the hard purities of symmetry and geometry, the forms never attain them.

Perched on these relaxed masses, the sticks and their shadows are abrupt and angular. The eggs are dramatic in their smooth perfection. Conspicuously unsculpted and pearl white, they accent by contrast the sensuousness of the gentle buildings they help sustain.

It is customary to apply the term vernacular to the great Sahelian mosques, notably Djenné (pl. 27-30). It is also not accurate, a sign that where a monumental tradition is little known outside Africa, it is easier to classify it as *folk* than to accept its sophistication and grandeur. As the world grows more familiar with the splendor of these mosques, their being called *vernacular* will probably be looked back on as having been naive.

Pl. 22-39. The dry savannah south of the Sahara features a unique style of mosque. The sculpted look of the older and more rural mosques is not due to weathering; molded contours are part of the original design.

Pl. 23

Pl. 24

Pl. 23. Sticks bristle from walls and towers, providing permanent scaffolding for maintenance. Pinnacles are often topped by ostrich eggs, symbols of fertility.

Pl. 25

Pl. 26

Pl. 27

Pl. 27-30. The Great Mosque at Djenné, Mali, built in 1907, is the most famous in West Africa. "Guardian pillars" to the right and left mark the graves of marabouts and entrances to the mosque's terrace.

Pl. 28

Pl. 30

Pl. 30. Market day.

ι most Sahelian mosques, aisles studded by massive columns form the entire interior space.

Pl. 29

Pl. 32

Pl. 31

Pl. 34

Pl. 33

Pl. 34. Crowning the corner of a mosque built in 1978, phallus and ostrich egg dramatically suggest generation.

PI. 37

PI. 36

PI. 35

Pl. 37. The eastern facade of the mosque at Niono is 160 feet long.

Pl. 38

Pl. 39

Pl. 39. In a village not far from Djenné, a recent example of the "Djenné style" is seen at its most severe.

Pl. 42. Hazara pilgrims at a ziarat.

Plates 40-52. In Afghanistan, the Muslim shrine, or ziarat, is as important as the mosque. Often marking the grave of saint, the ziarat commemorates and occasions miracles.

Pl. 44

Pl. 44. Pilgrims leave flags to remind the saint to intercede with God on their behalf. A main function of the ziarat is to restore and prolong good health.

Pl. 45

Pl. 46

Pl. 49. Two days in the ziarat cures many pilgrims of insanity.

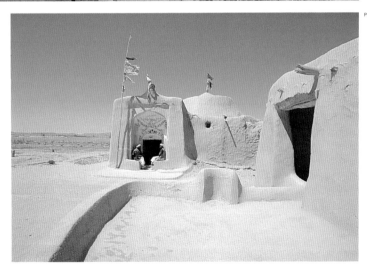

Pl. 47, 48. A ziarat near a city famous for having ninety-nine shrines.

PI. 51

PI. 50

Pl. 50-52. The ziarat often celebrates generativity and nurture with forms that mimic phallus and breast. Geometry relaxes into flesh.

PI. 52

ASKING THE GOOD AND STRONG: AFGHAN MUSLIM SHRINES

(plates 40-52)

In Afghanistan's dry, rugged landscape, down a long valley or high on a distant slope, a bright banner will often catch the eye. These vivid flags announce from afar the presence of a Muslim shrine, or *ziarat*.

Ziarat comes from an Arabic word meaning pilgrimage. Though frowned upon by the orthodox, such shrines are ancient and widespread in Islam. Often the graves of saints, they commemorate and occasion miracles. People implore the saints' spirits—the good and strong—to plead with God on their behalf.[1]

In Afghanistan, believers may leave a small, brightly colored cloth or piece of string to remind the saint of their prayer after their departure. Many larger cloths are ceremonially replaced at the spring equinox, which is the Afghan New Year.[2] A main function of the ziarat is to restore and prolong good health. Driving a nail into a special pole or tree can cure toothache. Dust from the site rubbed on a painful joint often relieves the anguish.

Special chambers cure insanity. To visit an important ziarat, pilgrims may travel hundreds of miles. Buildings for cooking and others for sleeping allow visitors to remain as long as they wish. A caretaker usually lives nearby.

The story of a small roadside shrine at Kalaikozi is typical of the thousands of ziarats which dot the Afghan countryside. About fifty miles north of Bamiyan, this shrine was built around 1920. It marks the spot where a man, exhausted from seeking help for his desperately ill brother, dismounted from his horse and briefly slept. It was broad daylight. When he awoke, a stranger approached on foot and handed him an apple. "Give this to your sick brother," he said, and kept on walking.

The man rushed home and administered the apple. Instantly the brother recovered. The stranger, the family realized, was Khoje Kheder, a spirit who sometimes rescues those in urgent need. Before Mohammed's time, Khoje Kheder drank from a spring of immortality. Invisible at will, he travels at once where he wishes. The sick man's family built the ziarat to express their gratitude. Others leave bits of cloth in the hope Khoje Kheder will help them.[3]

Afghanistan is "big" country. Landscape features are large-scale. The raw, sweeping grandeur undermines a sense of "here." Particularly in dry, sparsely inhabited mountains, the brilliant hue of ziarat banners fixes and celebrates place amid immensity.

In the village, too, the ziarat's visual function is striking. Partly to protect women from public view, traditional Afghan dwellings face interior courtyards surrounded by high walls. The house looks in, defends, excludes. By contrast, the ziarat beckons. It is open and affable. Its surrounding walls are almost always low. They mark space, rarely restrict it. The village ziarat's sociability is a visual gift to the traveler and a public expression of community.

Ziarat and mosque have different uses. By custom, women do not pray in the Afghan rural mosque. There, men alone affirm their faith in a unique, transcendent God. At the ziarat, women and men address a more local, personal spirit. Mosque and ziarat look different too. The mosque is generally a formal building, tending toward elegance and splendor. The classic, international tradition of the large mosques is the fruit of wealth and literacy.

But in the rural ziarat, geometric precision is conspicuously absent. No mechanical instrument has refined the efforts of eye and hand. The ziarat seems more molded than measured, more spontaneous than designed, more from the hand and heart than from the brain. Its scale is intimate. It sits rather than soars.

The ziarat long pre-dates Islam, which has incorporated it reluctantly. Basically an earth shrine, one of its key purposes is to grant fertility to the barren. As a kind of nature worship declared in *architecture parlante*, the ziarat often celebrates generativity and nurture with forms that mimic phallus and breast. Geometry relaxes into flesh. Bypassing the cool canons of urbanity, the ziarat's organic forms directly express reverence for the central energies of life.[4]

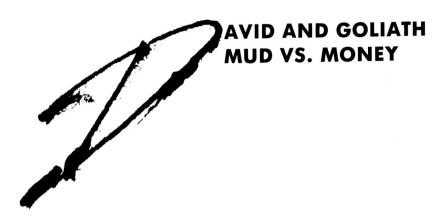

DAVID AND GOLIATH
MUD VS. MONEY

Western prejudice toward non-Western cultures has, in the last hundred years, declined. Many of us have learned the sensitivity to wince when hunter-gatherers are distinguished from rural farmers by being called "savages" rather than "barbarians."[1]

But a related civility masks arrogance. Consider calling societies or nations *pre-industrial*, *underdeveloped*, or *developing*, terms which have been widely adopted as economic euphemisms.[2] In pointing to the future, they redefine present *poverty* as imminent or eventual *wealth*. How gracious. The terms enshrine in our very language our optimism, even conviction, that the non-consuming world is upwardly mobile and shall, one day, join our club. This conceptual maneuver appropriates the future. Declaring it an industrial and post-industrial cornucopia, the tactic awards validity to the present in the degree to which "now" prefigures and prepares a "soon" or "someday" full of factories, vehicles, and computers. A less

value-laden term than "developing" would be "non-transformed."

Another word in common use is *subsistence*, as in "subsistence farming" or "subsistence economy." The term distinguishes societies without high capitalization or cash crops from ones whose market economies are growing. The usage is not neutral. Employed mostly by economists keen on maximizing systems—exchanges of materials, services, goods, and money—the term implies non-cooperative, shameful withdrawal, an inability to face and join a dynamic world. Further, the word suggests meagerness, a sense of barely enough, of hanging on to life with resources so fragile they deserve pity at best.

But a "subsistence" economy could be easily called "local," "independent," or "autonomous."[3] Isolated, self-sufficient villagers, introduced to simple manufactured goods such as mirrors, durable knives, and kitchen utensils, are

usually eager to acquire them. This desire is frequently presented as evidence that, free to choose, all traditional people "really prefer" modern ways. But as the geographer John Bodley points out, though "demand for these simple utilitarian articles often initiate[s] certain changes in tribal life, it do[es] not mean a rejection of traditional culture" in favor of modern economic roles.[4]

Between the industrialized world committed to high per-capita energy consumption and "growth," and the vernacular world, committed to a local, ecologically healthy society, there lies an enormous gap.[5] At one extreme, developmentalists work to close the gap. They seek to "elevate" the "backward" into the modern world. At the other extreme, traditionalists want to maintain the gap or even widen it, to insulate local cultures' rich individuality against the spread of homogenizing materialism.[6]

If these unmodified positions—assimilation and isolation—appear drastic, perhaps the responsible course is a middle one: integration. Maybe it is best to implement the faith of an anthropologist discussing tribal policy in India: "We believe that we can bring them the best things of our world without destroying the nobility and the goodness of theirs."[7]

The problem is that, in practice, this faith so often fails.[8] For example, in rural Africa and Asia, a family building or replacing a dwelling often substitutes cement for mud. Choosing so substantial a market item over a local one means real disruption. To raise the cash someone must leave the village to earn a wage—turn "industrial bachelor."[9]

Mud can be stabilized by adding relatively small amounts of cement or asphalt.[10] At first glance the process seems cheap and useful. To build with, say, 7% cement instead of the roughly 20% needed in most concrete seems a major economy. In fact, stabilized mud, for village dwellings at least, is expensive and redundant. Where in an industrialized country a poor person can buy ten bags of cement with one day's wages, in rural Africa ten days' work buys a single bag.[11] An average local family may as well yearn for a stabilized mud house as for the moon.[12] In addition, village housing in stabilized mud is unnecessary. Vernacular mud construction is quite adequate.[13]

In a controversy which has recently drawn wide attention, major manufacturers of infant formula have sought in the Third

World to identify their product with "progress." They claim that science's milk is more nutritious than mother's. Pursuaded, many Third World parents have become consumers. But insufficient cash often cruelly twists their best intentions. Diluting the formula to stretch it leads to malnutrition, and—to save fuel—skimping on or omitting sterilization causes disease. The risk of disease is increased by formula's inability to provide natural immunities transmitted in breast milk. Further, mothers dissatisfied with formula and wishing to nurse cannot. Their hormone systems read milk unsuckled as milk unneeded, and their breasts go dry.[14]

There are important parallels between selling formula to the Third World and selling cement. The first practice is far more cruel. But both are examples of self-serving technology redefining sufficiency as under-development. Free and abundant, milk and mud are declared inadequate, and industrial interests stand ready to provide expensive, artificial substitutes.

Like the woman using formula, the builder in cement requires professional training.[15] Nursing mother and the builder in mud need only vernacular—local—instruction. Both formula and cement are addictive. After an industrial fix, women cannot simply return to nursing. After a generation of cement, many villages lose their vernacular building skills. Dependence on the market, at first "voluntary," often cannot be reversed.[16]

Foolish glamor in architecture is anything but new. In the seventeenth century, the English poet Alexander Pope teased the mindless importation of architectural features appropriate to Italy's dry, hot climate into England, where the weather is cool and damp. He laughed at fashionable Englishmen "[p]roud to catch cold at a Venetian door."[17] He would laugh today at the desert dweller's cement house needing expensive air conditioning while "poor" neighbors live comfortably in mud.[18]

Traditional desert architecture can prompt languor or energy. In the first case, resigned to industrialization's advance, we focus on vernacular's poignancy and taste the sad pleasures of rue. Our interest is contemplative, sentimental, antiquarian. We imagine one more humane tradition crushed by development, the melancholy passing of yet one more impractical anachronism.

But in the second case, vernacular is seen as vital, not doomed. It inspires hope—resistance to the false, enervating myth that high technology shall triumph everywhere.[19] Cement's appeal is that it proclaims participation today in the progressive worldwide culture of tomorrow. But in fact cement is regressive. Since in most of the Third World there is an excess rather than a shortage of labor, the annual maintenance required by village construction in mud is not a problem. The shortage of capital is. Cement's finance, energy, water, and transportation costs are so high that its use in Third World deserts is conspicuous consumption.[20] More important, cement even scrupulously used is, in the desert, thermally inappropriate. Thin, it does not insulate, and occupants roast by day and shiver at night. Desert architecture needs to advance back to mud.

In the United States, people who practice *voluntary simplicity*—relaxation of the drive for high income and high consumption—tend to be of wealthy and middle-class backgrounds. Associating economy with want, the less affluent are less interested.[21] Must this pattern be repeated on a global basis? Or will more Third World leaders of vision arise like Julius Nyerere of Tanzania, who in 1977 spoke out against what he called ''European soil,'' or cement: ''The widespread addiction to cement and tin roofs is a kind of mental paralysis. We are still thinking in terms of international standards instead of what we can afford to do ourselves.''[22]

Mud is not a backward material that progress will replace. In the desert, vernacular, because profoundly local, is more efficient than centralized industrialization—more adaptive to local climate, local society, and local ecology. Mud's benefits are psychological, too. As a striking example of appropriate technology surpassing industrial, mud reduces neo-colonial dependence by promoting cultural self-respect.

The word *vernacular* has had a long, rich history. In Latin it originally meant ''whatever was homebred, homespun, homegrown, homemade, as opposed to what was obtained in formal exchange.'' Later, a Roman linguist applied the term's sense of ''produced locally'' to speech,[23] and in the seventeenth century English adapted this use. It was in 1857 that an architect, seeking to distinguish regional from academic, urbane styles, first applied vernacular to architecture.[24]

Recently, reviving vernacular's original economic meaning has been proposed.[25] This is a good idea. The word is a useful, non-technical way to refer to a whole range of autonomous activities, including architecture, which, rooted in local culture and ecology, escape the reach of bureaucrats, professionals, and the market. Among other benefits, recognition and defense of vernacular values would slow the flow of ecological refugees from countryside to city.

Shaken by environmental damage, increasing energy costs, and prolonged recession, the industrialized world is frightened as the dream of extravagance fades. Officially and emotionally identifying happiness with consumption, we fear that *appropriate technology* is a euphemism for degradation. Such fear deserves compassion, not vitriol. Vernacular architecture's beauty and ingenuity remind us that simplicity of means is not poverty of means. Its dignity reassures us that we can learn to overcome our dreams of greed and dominance, that we can grow past our illusion that wealth and power need to conquer nature.

Outside interest in desert vernacular architecture is very new. We are learning respect and gratitude for beauty which yesterday we ignored. But desert vernacular is more than lovely. It is also practical and ethical. With minimal means, it shelters against nature without abusing her.

Spiritually starved by the impersonal purities of modern architecture, many people are grateful to find in traditional desert structures the grace and splendor of the human touch. Mud makes gentle buildings—expressive, ecologically sound, humane. We are presently experiencing a shift in taste. Long neglected, vernacular desert architecture is at last finding its metaphorical, as well as physical, place in the sun.

The Image of The Desert

1. Antoine de Saint-Exupéry, *Terre des hommes* (1939) (Paris: Gallimard, 1979), p. 78.
2. See John K. Wright, ''Terrae Incognitae: The Place of the Imagination in Geography,'' in *Human Nature in Geography* (Cambridge: Harvard University Press, 1966), pp. 68-88.
3. E.W. Bovill, *The Golden Trade of the Moors*, (London: Oxford University Press, 1958).
4. W.D. Paden, *Tennyson in Egypt, A Study of the Imagery in His Earlier Work* (Lawrence, KS: University of Kansas, 1942), p. 141.
5. Between 1816 and 1824, three accounts of claimed visits to Timbuctoo were published in England, all dubious. The last was so outrageous it was actually a parody of the first two. Philip D. Curtin, *The Image of Africa, British Ideas and Action 1780-1850*, (Madison, WI: University of Wisconsin Press, 1964), pp. 164-165.
6. Alfred Lord Tennyson, *Timbuctoo*, lines 158-63, in *Tennyson, Selected Poetry*, ed. Douglas Bush (New York: Modern Library, 1951), pp. 6-12.
7. René Caillié, *Travels Through Central Africa to Timbuctoo*, 2 Vols. (London: Colburn and Bentley, 1830), 2:49.
8. Tennyson, *Timbuctoo*, lines 240-244.
9. D. Jacques-Meunié, *Cités anciennes de Mauritanie* (Paris: Klincksieck, 1961), pp. 71-75.
10. CRATerre/UPA de Grenoble, ''Terre: construire en terre crue dans les pays industrialisés,'' *Bulletin d'informations architecturales*, ENSBA-IFA (October 1981), p. 1.

Water, Snow, and Sand

1. James Marston Fitch, *American Building*, Vol. 2, *The Environmental Forces that Shape It* (Boston: Houghton Mifflin, 1972), pp. 266-71. Richard Stein, *Architecture & Energy* (Garden City, NY: Anchor, 1978), pp. 25-30, 37-39.
2. Antoine de Saint-Exupéry, *Wind, Sand, and Stars* (London: Pan, 1979), pp. 77-78.
3. One defense against ignorance is humor. One of our photographs of the Great Mosque drew the comment, ''Very nice—until the tide comes in.''
4. See CRATerre (P. Doat, et al), *Construire en terre* (Paris: Alternative et Parallèles, 1979). Also see *H, Revue de l'habitat social*, 66 (September 1981): 1-69, 94-95.
5. CRATerre, *Construire en terre*, p. 102.
6. Gaston Bachelard, *The Poetics of Space* (Boston: Beacon, 1969), p. 6.
7. On climatocentrism and attitudes toward nature, see Aldous Huxley, ''Wordsworth in the Tropics,'' in *Do What You Will* (London: Chatto and Windus, 1929), pp. 113-129.

Mud Stands Up: Construction Techniques

1. See Susan Denyer, *Traditional African Architecture* (New York: Africana, 1978), pp. 16-21, 31-35.
2. Labelle Prussin, ''Sudanese Architecture and the Manding,'' *African Arts*, Summer 1970, pp. 13-19, 64-67 [18 & 64].
3. For a detailed historical survey in Africa, see Labelle Prussin's Ph.D. dissertation, *The Architecture of Djenné: African Synthesis and Transformation* (Ann Arbor, MI: University Microfilms, 1974), pp. 117-54. Also see Franco Frescura, *Rural Shelter in Southern Africa*

(Johannesburg: Ravan, 1981). For a comprehensive, practical account of a wide variety of techniques, see CRATerre (P. Doat, et al), *Construire en terre*, (Paris: Alternative et Paralleles, 1979).

4. Richard Hughes, of the London chapter of the International Commission on Monuments and Sites (ICOMOS), is investigating the chemical and physical properties of vernacular mud recipes. His published findings will be of great interest.

5. Richard Day, "Rammed Earth," *Popular Science*, December 1981, pp. 114-17, 121-22. Richard Bender, "Dust to Dust," *Progressive Architecture*, December 1973, pp. 64-67.

6. David R. Lee, "Mud Mansions of Northern Sudan," *African Arts*, Autumn 1971, pp. 60-62, 84.

7. Sybil Moholy-Nagy, *Native Genius in Anonymous American Architecture* (New York: Schocken, 1976), p. 172.

8. See A.J. Spencer, *Brick Architecture in Ancient Egypt* (Warminster, England: Aris and Phillips, 1979), pp. 3-6.

9. Peter Nabokov, *Adobe: Pueblo and Hispanic Folk Traditions of the Southwest* (Washington: Office of Folklife Programs, Smithsonian Institution, 1981), p. 4.

Mud In Our Eyes

1. Christian Norberg-Schulz, *Genius Loci: Towards a Phenomenology of Architecture* (New York: Rizzoli, 1980), pp. 21, 45, 112-38.

2. The word *primitive* is used here with reluctance, even apology. It is used only because it is the best known of a range of poor alternatives. The term's advocates stress that to many people it is descriptive, not derogatory, and even connotes praise (see for example Paul S. Wingert, *Primitive Art: Its Traditions and Styles* (New York: Oxford, 1962), pp. 3-11 and Stanley Diamond, *In Search of the Primitive: A Critique of Civilization* (New Brunswick, NJ: Transaction, 1981), particularly chapter 4. But the claim that traditional societies necessarily precede ours in evolutionary time or in degree of complexity is ethnocentric and condescending. In addition, traditional societies themselves don't like to be called primitive, particularly by people whose values are more material than spiritual.

3. Robert Goldwater, *Primitivism in Modern Art* (New York: Random House, 1967), p. 87.

4. For Gropius' rejection of "primitive" architecture, see Joseph Rykwert, *On Adam's House In Paradise* (Cambridge: Massachusetts Institute of Technology Press, 1981), p. 24.

5. Henry-Russell Hitchcock, Jr., *Modern Architecture: Romanticism and Reintegration* (New York: Payson and Clark, 1929), p. 213.

6. For its former apotheosis, see Reyner Banham, *Theory and Design in the First Machine Age* (Cambridge: Massachusetts Institute of Technology Press, 1981).

7. See Lewis Mumford, *Technics and Civilization* (New York: Harcourt, Brace, & World, 1963) pp. 364-435.

8. See James S. Ackerman, "Transactions in Architectural Design," *Critical Inquiry*, 1:2 (December 1974), pp. 229-43; and Brent Brolin, *The Failure of Modern Architecture* (New York: Van Nostrand, Reinhold, 1976), pp. 55-56.

9. See Rykwert, *On Adam's House in Paradise*, p. 192.

10. Bernard Rudofsky, *Architecture Without Architects* (New York: Museum of Modern Art, 1965).

11. Bernard Rudofsky, *The Prodigious Builders* (New York: Harcourt Brace Jovanovitch, 1977), p. 368.

12. Although other architects were enthusiastic about specific vernaculars, Rudofsky was the first to gather many disparate examples and urge appreciation of the entire category. See Paul Oliver, "Attitudes in the Modern Movement," in Paul Oliver, ed. *Shelter and Society: Studies in Vernacular Architecture* (New York: Praeger, 1969), pp. 16-21.

13. James S. Ackerman, "The Demise of the Avant Garde: Notes on the Sociology of Recent American Art," *L'Arte*, 1969, pp. 5-17.

14. See Moshe Safdie, *Form and Purpose* (Boston: Houghton Mifflin, 1982), pp. 21-48.

15. Lionel Trilling, *Sincerity and Authenticity* (Cambridge: Harvard University Press, 1972), p. 100.

16. *Architecture Without Architects* was not reviewed by the *Journal of the Society of Architectural Historians*. (For a later rebuke of this omission, see John Maass, "Where Architectural Historians Fear to Tread," *JSAH*, 28 (March 1969): 3-8 [4]. It remained undiscussed in Amos Rapoport's seminal *House Form and Culture* (Englewood Cliffs, NJ: Prentice-Hall, 1969), was criticized by Paul Oliver for its "emphasis on the visual," in his "Attitudes in the Modern Movement," p. 21. and by Enrico Guidoni, *Primitive Architecture* (New York: Abrams, 1968), for its "formalism," p. 10.

17. For a concise discussion of this complex subject in relation to vernacular, see Paul Oliver, "Introduction" in Paul Oliver, ed., *Shelter, Sign, and Symbol* (Woodstock, NY: Overlook, 1977), pp. 7-37 [8-17]. The classic text is Amos Rapoport, *House Form and Culture*.

18. Susan Sontag, *On Photography* (New York: Delta, 1977), pp. 23, 24. For specific criticism of photography of vernacular, see P.G.

Anson, "Architecture Without Architects," *Landscape*, 12:2 (Winter, 1962-63), p. 18; and LaBelle Prussin, review of Rene Gardi, *Indigenous African Architecture,* in *African Arts*, 9:1 (October 1975), pp. 83-85.

19. Though a particularly open anthropologist would say no. See Robert Redfield, "Art and Icon," in Robert Redfield et al, *Aspects of Primitive Art* (New York: Museum of Primitive Art, 1959), pp. 11-40 [28].

20. See Carter Ratcliff, "American Indian Masterworks," *Art International*, 18:2 (February 1974), pp. 28-29, 52.

21. For example see Amos Rapoport, "An Approach to Vernacular Design," in James Marston Fitch, ed. *Shelter: Models of Native Ingenuity* (Katonah, NY: Katonah Gallery, 1982), pp. 43-48.

22. Oscar Wilde, "The Critic as Artist," in Richard Ellmann, ed. *The Artist as Critic: Critical Writings of Oscar Wilde,* (New York: Random House, 1969) p. 366.

23. See James S. Ackerman, "On Judging Art Without Absolutes," *Critical Inquiry* (Spring 1979), pp. 441-469 [441-449]. Also Stanford Anderson, "The Presentness of Interpretation and of Artifacts," in John E. Handcock, ed., *History in, of, and for Architecture* (Cincinnati: University of Cincinnati, 1981), pp. 49-57.

24. See Amos Rapoport, "Cross-Cultural Aspects of Environmental Design" in *Environment and Culture,* vol. 4 of *Human Behavior and Environment (Advances in Theory and Research),* ed. I. Altman, A. Rapoport and J.F. Wohlwill (New York: Plenum, 1980) pp. 7-46. Also see Amos Rapoport and Newton Watson, "Cultural Variability in Physical Standards," in Robert Gutman, ed. *People and Buildings* (New York: Basic Books, 1972), pp. 33-53.

25. Because the West has for some time been interested in primitive art, a "primitive criticism," though not widely accepted, does exist. See Robert Goldwater, "Judgments of Primitive Art, 1905-1965," in Daniel Biebuyck, ed., *Tradition and Creativity in Tribal Art* (Berkeley: University of California Press, 1969), pp. 24-41.

Walls and Roofs

1. D. Jacques-Meunié, *Cités anciennes de Mauritanie* (Paris: Klincksieck, 1961), pp. 108-11.

2. O. du Pigaudeau, "Contribution à l'étude du symbolisme dans le décor mural et l'artisanat de Walata," *Bulletin de l'Institut Français d'Afrique Noire*, Série B, 19:1, 2 (January-April 1957), pp. 137-83.

3. On the secrecy surrounding the patterns' meaning, see G.J. Duchemin, "A propos des décorations murales de Oualata," *Bulletin de l'Institut Français d'Afrique Noire*, Série B, 12:4 (October 1950), pp. 1095-1110. The decoration will be discussed in Labelle Prussin's forthcoming book, *Hatumere: Islamic Design in West Africa* (Berkeley: University of California Press).

4. For a fuller description of Kachchhi architecture, see Jean-Louis Bourgeois and Carollee Pelos, "Mud, Mirrors, and Lime," *Architectural Review*, 162:1026 (August 1982), pp. 65-68. Also see Kulbhushan Jain, "Form, a Consequence of Context," *Process Architecture*, 15 (1980): 17-34; and Mayank Shah, "Nomadic Movements and Settlements of the Rabaris of Kutch," *Process Architecture*, 15 (1980): 49-66.

5. Elizabeth Beazley, "The Pigeon Towers of Isfahan," *Iran*, 4 (1966): 105-9.

6. Hans E. Wulff, *The Traditional Crafts of Persia: Their Development, Technology, and Influence on Eastern and Western Civilizations,* (Cambridge: Massachusetts Institute of Technology Press, 1966), p. 270.

7. Jane Dieulafoy, *La Perse, la Chaldée, et la Susiane,* (Paris, 1887), pp. 285-86.

8. Beazley, "The Pigeon Towers of Isfahan," p. 105.

9. Arthur Upham Pope, *A Survey of Persian Art,* (London: Oxford, 1939), vol. 2, p. 1200.

10. For the suggestion that, in the area, flat-roofed, rectangular houses have been built since at least the thirteenth century, see Tor Engstrom, *Notes sur les modes de construction au Soudan* Statens Etnografiska Museum Memoirs, 26 (Stockholm: Statens Etnografiska Museum, 1957), pp. 17-22, 34.

11. For modern application of the same principle see Allan Konya *Design Primer for Hot Climates* (London: Architectural Press, 1980), p.45.

12. Labelle Prussin, "Pillars, Projections, and Paradigms," *Architectura*, 7:1 (1977), pp. 65-72.

13. See Vinod Gupta, *Natural Cooling of Buildings* (Greenbelt, MD: Innovative Informations, 1981), pp. 7, 21, 23 and Richard G. Stein, *Architecture and Energy* (Garden City, NY: Anchor, 1978), pp. 31-33.

14. Labelle Prussin, "An Introduction to Indigenous African Architecture," in *Journal of the Society of Architectural Historians*, 33:3, (October 1974), pp. 183-205.

15. For a description and photos of such vaults being built in Egypt, see Hassan Fathy, *Architecture for the Poor* (Chicago: University of Chicago Press, 1973), pp. 6-11, illus. 7-18.

Wind and Ventilation

1. Joseph Needham, *Science and Civilization in China*, vol. 1. (Cambridge: Cambridge University Press, 1961), pp. 240-45; vol. 4 (Cambridge: Cambridge University Press, 1965), p. 556.

2. For an early account, see William Muir, *The Caliphate: Its Rise, Decline and Fall* (London, 1891), pp. 194-95.

3. Klaus Ferdinand, ''The Horizontal Windmills of Western Afghanistan,'' *Folk*, 5 (1963), pp. 71-89 [71]. Also see Ferdinand, *Folk* 8-9 (1966-67), pp. 83-88.

4. Paul Oliver, ''The Windmills of Murcia,'' in *Shelter* (Bolinas, CA: Shelter, 1973), p. 166.

5. The chronicler was Al-Masudi. Quoted in R.J. Forbes, ''Power,'' in Charles Singer et al, eds., *A History of Technology*, vol. 2, (Oxford: Clarendon, 1956), p. 616. Early accounts describe two different ways of using the wind to shift enormous quantities of sand. See Forbes, *Studies in Ancient Technology* (Leiden, Holland: Brill, 1965), vol. 2, p. 116; and Muhammed Dimashsqi, *Manuel de la cosmographie du moyen age,* trans. A.F. Mehren (Copenhagen, 1874), p. 247.

6. Dimashqi, *Manuel de la cosmographie*, pp. 246-47 and E. Aubert de la Rue, *Man and the Winds* (London: Hutchinson, 1955), pp. 194-95.

7. Hans E. Wulff, *The Traditional Crafts of Persia: Their Development, Technology, and Influence on Eastern and Western Civilizations*, (Cambridge: Massachusetts Institute of Technology Press, 1966), p. 288.

8. Ernest Ayscoghe Floyer, *Unexplored Baluchistan* (1882; Quetta, Pakistan: Gosha-e-Adab, 1977), pp. 321-22.

9. They face northwest. See Stanley Ira Hallet and Rafi Samizay, *Traditional Architecture of Afghanistan* (New York: Garland, 1980), pp. 154-55, 160-61.

10. Hassan Fathy, *Architecture for the Poor* (Chicago: University of Chicago Press, 1973), pp. 47-48. For other wind devices in Egypt see George Michell, ed. *Architecture of the Islamic World* (New York: William Morrow, 1978), pp. 179, 203.

11. Mohammed S. Elbadawi, ''Sahara'' in *Canadian Architect*, April 1972, pp. 63-66, and May 1972, pp. 55-59.

12. For photographs, see Jean-Louis Bourgeois and Carollee Pelos ''Mirrors, Mud, and Lime,'' *Architectural Review*, 162:1026 (August 1982), pp. 65-68.

13. Henry Pottinger, *Travels in Baloochistan and Sind* (London, 1816; Karachi: Indus, 1976), p. 354. Also see M.M. Menon, ''The City of Windcatchers,'' *Pakistan Quarterly* 7:4 (1957), pp. 14-17.

14. For a photograph, see Jean-Louis Bourgeois and Carollee Pelos, ''Sind Wind,'' *Architects' Journal*, 171:11 (12 March 1980), pp. 506-7.

15. For multi-storied examples in Iraq, see Subhi Hussein Al-Azzawi, ''Oriental Houses in Iraq,'' in *Shelter and Society,* ed. Paul Oliver (New York: Praeger, 1969), pp. 91-102.

16. Mehdi, N. Bahodori, ''Passive Cooling Systems in Iranian Architecture,'' *Scientific American* 238:2 (February 1978), pp. 144-154. Elizabeth Beazley, ''Some Vernacular Buildings of the Iranian Plateau,'' *Iran*, 15 (1977), pp. 89-102 [100-01]. Elizabeth Beazley and Michael Harverson, *Living With the Desert: Working Buildings of the Iranian Plateau* (Warminster: Aris and Phillips, forthcoming).

17. Allan Konya, *Design Primer for Hot Climates* (London: Architectural Press, 1980), p. 52. Incidentally, for a high-technology design where the stack effect drives a horizontal windmill, see Steven Vogel, ''Organisms That Capture Currents,'' *Scientific American*, August 1978, pp. 128-139 [139].

18. The waste is used as fertilizer. A hole is dug through the outside wall, then plugged and plastered. This recycling system is also used south of the Sahara, in Djenné (fig. 25) and as far east as Afghanistan. Also see David Etherton, ''Algerian Oases,'' in *Shelter in Africa*, Paul Oliver, ed. (London: Barrie & Jenkins, 1971), pp. 172-89 [188].

19. See Bernard Rudofsky, *The Prodigious Builders* (New York: Harcourt Brace Jovanovitch, 1977), pp. 20-47. For Tunisia, see David Aradeon, *African Architectural Technology* (catalogue), (Lagos, Nigeria: Second World Black and African Festival of Arts and Culture 1977), p. 10. For China, see Fenghuo Brigade, ''Fenghuo Production Brigade,'' *Mimar* 3 (January-March 1982): 28-31; Paul Sun, ''Underground Houses,'' *Mimar* 3, (January-March 1982): 42-47; and Mildred F. Schmertz, ''Islamic Architecture and Rural Dwellings from Beijing to Kashi,'' *Architectural Record* (May 1982), pp. 92-101.

20. For examples in Oualata, Mauritania, see Susan Denyer, *Traditional African Architecture* (New York: Africana, 1978), illus. 261, p. 169. Also observed first-hand 1980.

21. Rudofsky, *Prodigious Builders*, p. 289.

22. Rudofsky, *Prodigious Builders*, p. 288.

23. In 1975 a prominent architect snickered at the idea of adding a wind-catcher to an air-conditioned building. (Stanley Abercrombie, ''The Middle East: Design, Politics and Policy,'' *Design and Environment*, 6:4 (Winter 1975), pp. 10-33 [12]. But times change and energy costs have soared. Theoharis David, of David and Dikaios

Associates and Chairman of Graduate Architecture, Pratt Institute, has included a wind-catcher system in an air-conditioned office building, the Universal Tower now under construction in Nicosia, Cyprus. An entire issue of *Alternative Sources of Energy,* Number 56 (1982), is devoted to energy-efficient cooling techniques. Also see Number 57 (1982), p. 4.

Sacred Mud: Sahelian Mosques

1. Paul Bohannan and Philip Curtin, *Africa and Africans* (Garden City, NY: The Natural History Press, 1971), pp. 237-38.
2. Roland Oliver and J.D. Fage, *A Short History of Africa,* (Baltimore: Penguin, 1969), p. 90.
3. Labelle Prussin, ''The Architecture of Islam in West Africa,'' *African Arts,* 1:2 (Winter 1968), pp. 32-35, 70-74.
4. Batty ould Mbouya; interview, Oualata, December 1980.
5. See Labelle Prussin, ''Pillars, Projections, and Paradigms,'' in *Architectura,* 7:1 (1977), pp. 65-81.
6. Labelle Prussin, Ph.D. dissertation, *The Architecture of Djenné: African Synthesis and Transformation* (Ann Arbor, MI: University Microfilms, 1974), p. 23.

Asking the Good and Strong: Afghan Muslim Shrines

1. Louis Dupree, ''Saint Cults in Afghanistan,'' *American Universities Field Staff Reports,* 20:1 (LD-1-1976), 1976.
2. Louis Dupree, *Afghanistan* (Princeton: Princeton University Press, 1972).
3. This account was told to us in March 1979 by the son of the man to whom Khoje Kheder appeared.
4. For more photographs of ziarats, see Jean-Louis Bourgeois and Carollee Pelos, ''Afghan Muslim Shrines,'' *Architectural Review,* 168:1006, (December 1980), pp. 367-69. Incidentally, photograph 3 in that article is incorrectly labeled. It should read ''quintuple domed shrine in the Dasht Amiran, near Zaranj.''

David and Goliath: Mud vs. Money

1. See Joseph Rykwert, *On Adam's House in Paradise* (Cambridge: Massachusetts Institute of Technology Press, 1981), p. 15. The language was V. Gordon Childe's.
2. See Ivan Illich, *Shadow Work* (Salem, NH: Marion Boyars, 1981), p. 15.
3. See Lewis Mumford, *The Myth of the Machine,* vol. 2 *The Pentagon of Power* (New York: Harcourt Brace Jovanovich, 1970), pp. 400-404.

4. John H. Bodley, *Victims of Progress* (Menlo Park, CA: Benjamin/Cummings, 1975), p. 130.
5. See George Dalton, ''Theoretical Issues in Economic Anthropology,'' *Current Anthropology,* 10:1 (February 1969), pp. 63-89; also in George Dalton, ed. *Economic Development and Social Change: The Modernization of Village Communities* (Garden City, NY: Natural History Press, 1971), pp. 178-225.
6. For eloquence on this subject, see Shelly Kellman, ''The Yanomamis: Their Battle for Survival,'' *Journal of International Affairs,* 36:1 (Spring/Summer 1982), pp. 15-42 [41-42]. Toward analysis, see annotated ''Bibliography on commodity-intensive versus subsistence 'economies' '' in Illich, *Shadow Work,* pp. 126-27.
7. Quoted in Bodley, *Victims of Progress,* p. 167.
8. Ibid. pp. 149-167.
9. See Jean-Paul Bourdier, ''Genius Before Industry,'' *Progressive Architecture,* August 1982, pp. 54-59 [56-58].
10. Kelly Jon Morris, ''Cinva-Ram,'' in *Shelter,* (Bolinas, CA: Shelter Publications, 1973), p. 68. Incidentally, stabilizing mud may lower its thermal benefit. Mud's insulating effect depends almost directly on its thickness. If the strength cement adds tempts the builder to build thinner, say one brick thick instead of two, thermal lag—the hours the structure stays cool after sunrise and warm after sunset—will diminish sharply. (William Lumpkins, ''A Distinguished Architect Writes on Adobe,'' in *El Palacio* 77:4 (1972), p. 6).
11. Lloyd Timberlake, ''Mud Can Make It,'' *Development Forum,* 9:7 (September 1981), p. 6.
12. See Anil Agarwal, ''Let Them Live in Mud,'' *New Scientist,* 96:36 (16 December 1982), pp. 737-747 [746-747].
13. Hassan Fathy, a major Egyptian architect who pioneered the application of lessons learned from vernacular makes a point relevant around the world: ''Really low-cost housing must not need non-existent resources; mud-brick houses are today made all over Egypt without the help of machines and engineers, and we must resist the temptation to improve on something that is already satisfactory.'' (Hassan Fathy, *Architecture for the Poor* (Chicago: University of Chicago Press, 1973), p. 134.
14. See *New Internationalist,* no. 110 (April 1982), entire issue.
15. Inaccuracies result in defective shelter—concrete impurely mixed or improperly cast will set badly and, in the desert's temperature extremes, will be particularly liable to crack. See Brent Brolin, *The Failure of Modern Architecture* (New York: Van Nostrand, Reinhold, 1976), p. 105.

16. The story of infant formula is of course deeply sad. But one of its aspects is hopeful, too. In 1981, the World Health Organization adopted guidelines to restrict the aggressive marketing of formula. Though the WHO policy may still be weak and difficult to enforce, the example of its passage is important evidence that international social limits can be imposed on inhumane economic growth. Perhaps it is not utopian to imagine cement one day, if not restricted, at least challenged. More effective of course will be local refusal to buy cement and its accompanying heavy cultural baggage.

17. Alexander Pope, *Epistle to Burlington*, line 36, quoted in David Watkin, *Morality and Architecture* (Oxford: Clarendon, 1977), p. 12.

18. Hassan Fathy has enjoyed telling the following story: In a Third World desert capital, so much sun poured through an office's glass wall that, despite the air-conditioning, an important government official had to shift his desk to a cooler corridor. His department? The Building Research Center. (Fathy lecture at Columbia University, May 4, 1978). It is rare that an investigator so perfectly integrates desk and field studies. For its traditional houses duplicated in modern materials and a tribe's decision to move out and build as before, see David Aradeon, "Space and House Form: Teaching Cultural Significance to Nigerian Students," *Journal of Architectural Education*, 35:1 (Fall 1981), pp. 25-27.

19. For a discussion and debunking of this myth in relation to architecture, see Watkin, *Morality and Architecture,* pp. 9-11.

20. It is sometimes used as a plaster to veneer mud walls. In the U.S. Southwest, this practice is finally recognized as damaging the walls it is intended to protect. See Lumpkins, "A Distinguished Architect Writes on Adobe," pp. 2-10; Nory Miller, "Back to Basics," *Progressive Architecture*, 52:11 (November 1981), pp. 82-85; and Terrence Moore, "Treasures of the Southwest," *Historic Preservation,* 34:4 (July/August 1982) p. 38.

21. Duane Elgin, *Voluntary Simplicity* (New York: Bantam, 1981), p. 25.

22. Quoted in Jean Dethier, *Des architectures de terre* (Paris: Centre de Création Industrielle, 1981), p. 12.

23. Illich, *Shadow Work*, p. 57; also see pp. 24 & 132.

24. See Richard M. Candee, "American Vernacular Architecture," *Journal of the Society of Architectural Historians*, 24:4 (December 1975), pp. 302-03 [302]. For definitions of "vernacular" architecture, see Amos Rapoport, *House Form and Culture*, (Englewood Cliffs, NJ: Prentice-Hall, 1969), pp. 2-8; Paul Oliver, "Introduction" in Paul Oliver, ed., *Shelter, Sign, and Symbol* (Woodstock, NY: Overlook, 1977), pp. 12-13; and Amos Rapoport, "An Interview with Amos Rapoport on Vernacular Architecture," *M.E.T.U. Journal of the Faculty of Architecture,* 5:2 (Fall 1979), pp. 114-116. See also Christopher Alexander, *Notes on the Synthesis of Form* (Cambridge: Harvard University Press, 1966), pp. 30-36; and Dr. Jay Edwards, ed., *The Study of Vernacular Architecture* (Baton Rouge: Louisiana State University Press, forthcoming).

Unless otherwise noted, all photographs from North and West Africa were taken 1980-81 and from Asia, 1978-79.

Frontispiece. House in Djenné, Mali.

The Image of the Desert
Figures

1. Dhoravira village, Kachchh, Gujarat State, India
2. Small mosque overlooking Hindu Kush mountains near Bamiyan, Afghanistan

Plates

1. The Red City overlooks the Bamiyan Valley, Afghanistan
2. Tamilout village, Atlas Mountains, Morocco
3. The town of Oualata, Mauritania, West Africa
4. A mild sandstorm, Nema, Mauritania

Mud Stands Up: Construction Techniques
Plates

5. Making mud bricks with a double mold in southern Morocco
6. Mud bricks drying in the sun, Bost, Afghanistan
7. The "rammed earth" or pisé method of construction near Erfoud, Morocco
8. Interior wall decoration being applied in Janan, Gujarat State, India
9. Granaries in Affala, Niger, West Africa
10. Incising a pattern on a courtyard wall, Oualata, Mauritania
11. Annual replastering of an exterior wall, Djenné, Mali

Walls and Roofs
Figure

3. Dwelling in Djenné, Mali

Plates

12-19. Five dwellings in Oualata, Mauritania
20, 21. Two dwellings in Janan, Gujarat State, India

Figures

4-7 A Rabari caste house, interior; Gado, India (photo 1981).
8, 9. A pigeon tower near Isfahan, Iran
10. Dwelling in Enghem, Mali
11. Dwelling c. 1974 in Enghem, Mali
12, 13. Two dwellings in Aoré, Mali
14, 15. Two Young Men's Houses, both c. 1970, in Aoré, Mali
16. A dwelling, 1980, in Aoré, Mali
17, 18. Multiple dwellings in Sebi, Mali
19. Dwelling in Aoré, Mali
20. Dwelling in Kotaka, Mali
21. Dwelling 1980, in Aoré, Mali
22. An entry house, 1973, in Bia, Mali
23. A Young Men's House in Bia, Mali
24. Dwelling in Djenné, Mali
25. Dwelling in Djenné, Mali. The massive column is topped by a toilet.
26. Dwelling in Djenné, Mali
27. A holy man's house, built before 1925 in Ségou, Mali
28. Dwelling, c. 1980, in Tourime, Senegal
29-35. Seven dwellings, c. 1970-1980, in Diado, Mali

36. Young Men's House, c. 1950 in Kolenze, Mali. Sculptor: Bakomani Yena
37, 38. Dwelling in Waounde, Senegal
39, 40. Dwelling, 1949, in Waounde, Senegal
41. Dwelling, c. 1950, in Verma, Senegal
42. A small mosque, 1942, in Affala, Niger
43. An entry house, c. 1960, in Affala, Niger
44. ''Hausa dome'' of an entry house, c. 1935, in Tahoua, Niger
45. Dome in a dwelling, Bamiyan, Afghanistan
46. Townscape in Jowain, Afghanistan

47,48. Shrine of Mlano Baba, c. 1860, southwest of Ghazni, Afghanistan
49. Shrine of Khoje Sandur in Doab, Afghanistan
50, 51. Shrine in the Dasht-Amiran near Zaranj, Afghanistan
52. Shrine of Doazda Emam, Hrasrud, Afghanistan

Drawings and Plan by Mark Truman

Maps by Kate Thom

Wind and Ventilation
Figures

47, 48. A windmill for grinding grain, c. 1960, in Jowain, Afghanistan
49-51. Wind-catchers in Tatta, Pakistan
52,53. Dwelling, c. 1960, with large wind-catchers in Tatta, Pakistan
54. A lane, near Erfoud, Morocco
55. Light-wells in covered street, Maadid, Morocco
56, 57. Dwelling in Maadid, Morocco
58. Cooling device on a dwelling, Janan village, Gujarat State, India

Sacred Mud: Sahelian Mosques
Plates

22. A small mosque, c. 1960, in Niono, Mali
23-26. Mosque, 1935, at San, Mali
27-30. The Great Mosque, 1907, of Djenné, Mali
31,32. Mosque, 1917?, at Point A, Mali
33,34. Mosque, 1978, in Dahelan, Mali
35-37. The largest mosque, c. 1957-58, in Niono, Mali
38. Mosque in Sanse, Mali
39. Mosque, 1981, Titama, Mali

Asking the Good and Strong: Afghan Muslim Shrines
Plates

40,41. The shrine of Mir Sayid Ali Yakhsuz, Bamiyan, Afghanistan
42. Hazara pilgrims in Doab, Afghanistan
43. The shrine of Mir Ashim Agha in Bamiyan, Afghanistan
44,45. The shrine of Sayid Merza Khoja, descendent of Abubakr Sidikh; c. 1730, Tala, Afghanistan
46. Pushtun pilgrims in Doab, Afghanistan.

Abercrombie, Stanley. "The Middle East: Design, Politics and Policy," *Design and Environment*, 6:4 (Winter 1975), pp. 10-33.

Ackerman, James S. "The Demise of the Avant Garde: Notes on the Sociology of Recent American Art," *L'Arte* (1969), pp. 5-17.

_____. "On Judging Art Without Absolutes," *Critical Inquiry*, (Spring 1979), pp. 441-469.

_____. "Transactions in Architectural Design," *Critical Inquiry*, 1:2 (December 1974), pp. 229-243.

Agarwal, Anil. "Let Them Live in Mud," *New Scientist*, 96:36 (16 December 1982), pp. 737-747.

Al-Azzawi, Subhi Hussein. "Oriental Houses in Iraq," in Paul Oliver, ed., *Shelter and Society*. New York: Praeger, 1969, pp. 91-102.

Alexander, Christopher. *Notes on the Synthesis of Form*. Cambridge: Harvard University Press, 1966.

Alternative Sources of Energy, Nos. 56 and 57 (1982).

Anderson, Stanford. "The Presentness of Interpretation and of Artifacts," in John E. Hancock, ed., *History in, of, and for Architecture. Cincinnatti: University of Cincinnatti, 1981, pp. 49-57.*

Anson, P.G. "Architecture Without Architects," Landscape, 12:2 (Winter 1962-63), p. 18.

Aradeon, David. "African Architectural Technology" (catalogue). Lagos, Nigeria: Second World Black and African Festival of Arts and Culture (1977).

_____. "Space and House Form: Teaching Cultural Significance to Nigerian Students," *Journal of Architectural Education*, 35:1 (Fall 1981), pp. 25-27.

Aubert de la Rue, E. *Man and the Winds*. London: Hutchinson, 1955.

Bachelard, Gaston. *The Poetics of Space*. Boston: Beacon, 1969.

Bahodori, Mehdi N. "Passive Cooling Systems in Iranian Architecture," *Scientific American*, 238:2 (February 1978), pp. 144-154.

Banham, Reyner. *Theory and Design in the First Machine Age*. Cambridge: Massachusetts Institute of Technology Press, 1981.

Beazley, Elizabeth. "The Pigeon Towers of Isfahan," *Iran* (1966) 4:105-109.

_____. "Some Vernacular Buildings of the Iranian Plateau," *Iran* (1977) 15:89-102.

Beazley, Elizabeth and Harverson, Michael. *Living With the Desert: Working Buildings of the Iranian Plateau*. Warminster: Aris and Phillips, forthcoming.

Bender, Richard. "Dust to Dust," *Progressive Architecture* (December 1973), pp. 64-67.

Bodley, John H. *Victims of Progress*. Menlo Park, CA: Benjamin/Cummings, (1975).

Bohannan, Paul and Curtin, Philip. *Africa and Africans*. Garden City, NY: The Natural History Press, 1971.

Bourdier, Jean-Paul. "Genius Before Industry," *Progressive Architecture* (August 1982), pp. 54-59.

Bourgeois, Jean-Louis and Pelos, Carollee. "Afghan Muslim Shrines," *Architectural Review*, 168:1006 (December 1980), pp. 367-69.

_____. "Mud, Mirrors, and Lime," *Architectural Review*, 172:1026 (August 1982), pp. 65-68.

_____. "Sind Wind," *Architects' Journal*, 171:11 (12 March 1980), pp. 506-7.

Bovill, E.W. *The Golden Trade of the Moors*. London: Oxford University Press, 1958.

Brolin, Brent. *The Failure of Modern Architecture*. New York: Van Nostrand, Reinhold, 1976.

Caillié, René. *Travels Through Central Africa to Timbuctoo*. London: Colburn and Bentley, 1830. 2 vols.; vol 2, p. 49.

Candee, Richard M. "American Vernacular Architecture," *Journal of the Society of Architectural Historians*, 34:4 (December 1975), pp. 302-03.

CRATerre (P. Doat, A. Hays, H. Houben, S. Matuk, F. Vitoux) *Construire en terre*. Paris: Alternative et Paralleles, 1979.

CRATerre/UPA de Grenoble. "Terre: construire en terre crue dans les pays industrialisés," *Bulletin d'informations architecturales*, supplément au no. 61 (October 1981).

Curtin, Philip D. *The Image of Africa: British Ideas and Action 1780-1850*. Madison, WI: University of Wisconsin Press, 1964.

Dalton, George. "Theoretical Issues in Economic Anthropology," *Current Anthropology*, 10:1 (February 1969), pp. 63-69. Also in George Dalton, ed., *Economic Development and Social Change: The Modernization of Village Communities*. Garden City, NY: Natural History Press, 1971, pp. 178-225.

Day, Richard. "Rammed Earth," *Popular Science* (December 1981), pp. 114-117, 121-122.

Denyer, Susan. *Traditional African Architecture*. New York: Africana, 1978.

Dethier, Jean. *Des architectures de terre*. Paris: Centre de Creation Industrielle, 1981, p. 12.

Diamond, Stanley. *In Search of the Primitive: A Critique of Civilization*. New Brunswick, NJ: Transaction, 1981.

Dieulafoy, Jane. *La Perse, la Chaldée, et la Susiane*. Paris, 1887.

Dimashqi, Muhammed. *Manuel de la cosmographie du moyen age*. Translated by A.F. Mehren. Copenhagen, 1874.

Du Pigaudeau, O. "Contribution à l'étude du symbolisme dans le décor mural et l'artisanat de Walata," *Bulletin de L'Institut Français d'Afrique Noire*, Série B, Nos. 1-2 (January-April 1957), 19:137-183.

Duchemin, G.J. "A propos des décorations murales de Oualata," *Bulletin de L'Institut Français d' Afrique Noire*, Série B, 12:4 (October 1950), pp. 1095-1110.

Dupree, Louis. *Afghanistan*. Princeton: Princeton University Press, 1973.

_____. "Saint Cults in Afghanistan," *American Universities Field Staff Reports*, 20:1 (1976).

Edwards, Jay D. *The Study of Vernacular Architecture*. Baton Rouge: Louisiana State University Press, forthcoming.

Elbadawi, Mohammed S. "Sahara," in *Canadian Architect*, April 1972, pp. 63-66 and May 1972, pp. 55-59.

Elgin, Duane. *Voluntary Simplicity*. New York: Bantam, 1982.

Engstrom, Tor. *Notes sur les modes de construction au Soudan*, Statens Etnografiska Museum Memoir 26. Stockholm: Statens Etnografiska Museum, 1957.

Etherton, David. "Algerian Oases," in Paul Oliver, ed., *Shelter in Africa*. London: Barrie and Jenkins, 1971, pp. 172-189.

Fathy, Hassan. *Architecture for the Poor*. Chicago: University of Chicago Press, 1973.

Fenghuo Brigade. "Fenghuo Production Brigade," *Mimar* 3 (January-March 1982), pp. 28-31.

Ferdinand, Klaus. "The Horizontal Windmills of Western Afghanistan," *Folk*, 5 (1963), pp. 71-89.

_____. "The Horizontal Windmills of Western Afghanistan: An Additional Note," *Folk*, 8-9 (1966-67), pp. 83-88.

Fitch, James Marston. *American Building*, 2 vols.; vol. 2, *The Environmental Forces That Shape It*. Boston: Houghton Mifflin, 1972.

Floyer, Ernest Ayscoghe. *Unexplored Baluchistan*. 1882; Quetta, Pakistan: Gosha-e-Adab, 1977.

Forbes, R.J. "Power," in Charles Singer, et al, eds., *A History of Technology*, vol. 2, Oxford: Clarendon, 1956.

_____. *Studies in Ancient Technology*. Leiden, Holland: Brill, 1965.

Frescura, Franco. *Rural Shelter in Southern Africa*. Johannesburg: Ravan, 1981.

Gardi, René. *Indigenous African Architecture*. New York: Van Nostrand Reinhold, 1974.

Goldwater, Robert. "Judgments of Primitive Art, 1905-1965," in Daniel Biebuyck, ed., *Tradition and Creativity in Tribal Art*. Berkeley: University of California Press, 1969, pp. 24-41.

_____. *Primitivism in Modern Art*. New York: Random House, 1967.

Guidoni, Enrico. *Primitive Architecture*. New York: Abrams, 1978.

Gupta, Vinod. *Natural Cooling of Buildings*. Greenbelt, MD: Innovative Informations, 1981.

Hallet, Stanley Ira and Samizay, Rafi. *Traditional Architecture of Afghanistan*. New York: Garland, 1980.

H, Revue de l'habitat social, 66 (September 1981), pp. 1-69, 94-95.

Hitchcock, Jr., Henry-Russell. *Modern Architecture: Romanticism and Reintegration*. New York: Payson and Clark, 1929.

Huxley, Aldous. "Wordsworth in the Tropics," in *Do What You Will*. London: Chatto and Windus, 1923.

Illich, Ivan. *Shadow Work*. Salem, NH: Marion Boyars, 1981.

Jacques-Meunié, D. *Cités anciennes de la Mauritanie*. Paris: Klincksieck, 1961.

Jain, Kulbhushan. "Form, a Consequence of Context," *Process Architecture*, 15 (1980), pp. 17-34.

Kellman, Shelly. "The Yanomamis: Their Battle for Survival," *Journal of International Affairs*, 36:1 (Spring/Summer 1982), pp. 15-42.

Konya, Allan. *Design Primer for Hot Climates*. London: Architectural Press, 1980.

Lee, David R. "Mud Mansions of Northern Sudan," *African Arts* (Autumn 1971), pp. 60-62, 84.

Lowenthal, David. "Geography, Experience, and Imagination: Toward a Geographical Epistemology," *Annals of the Association of American Geographers*, 51 (1961), pp. 241-260.

Lumpkins, William. "A Distinguished Architect Writes on Adobe," in *El Palacio*, 77:4 (1972), pp. 2-10.

Maybury-Lewis, David. "Societies on the Brink," *Harvard Magazine* (January-February, 1977), pp. 56-61.

Mekkawi, Mod. *Bibliography on Traditional Architecture in Africa*. Arlington, VA: Published by author, 1979.

Menon, M.M. "The City of Windcatchers," *Pakistan Quarterly*, 7:4 (1957), pp. 14-17.

Michell, George, ed., *Architecture of the Islamic World*. New York: William Morrow, 1978.

Miller, Nory. "Back to Basics," *Progressive Architecture*, 52:11 (November 1981), pp. 82-85.

Moholy-Nagy, Sybil. *Native Genius in Anonymous American Architecture*. New York: Schocken, 1976.

Moore, Terrence. "Treasures of the Southwest," *Historic Preservation*, 34:4 (July/August 1982), pp. 38-43.

Morris, Kelly Jon. "Cinva-Ram," in *Shelter*. Bolinas, CA: Shelter, 1973.

Muir, William. *The Caliphate: Its Rise, Decline and Fall*. London: 1891.

Mumford, Lewis. *The Myth of the Machine*, 2 vols.; vol. 2, *The Pentagon of Power*. New York: Harcourt Brace World, 1963.

Nabokov, Peter. *Adobe: Pueblo and Hispanic Folk Traditions of the Southwest*. Washington: Office of Folklife Programs, Smithsonian Institution, 1981.

Needham, Joseph. *Science and Civilization in China*. Vol. 1. Cambridge: Cambridge University Press, 1961. Vol. 4, 1965.

New Internationalist (England). April, 1982.

Norberg-Schulz, Christian. *Genius Loci: Towards a Phenomenology of Architecture*. New York: Rizzoli, 1980.

Oliver, Paul. "Attitudes in the Modern Movement" in Paul Oliver, ed., *Shelter and Society: Studies in Vernacular Architecture*. New York: Praeger, 1975, pp. 16-21.

_____, ed., *Shelter in Africa*. London: Barrie and Jenkins, 1971.

_____. Introduction to *Shelter, Sign, and Symbol*. Woodstock, NY: Overlook, 1977, pp. 7-37.

_____. "The Windmills of Murcia," in *Shelter*. Bolinas, CA: Shelter, 1973, p. 166.

Oliver, Roland, and Fage, J.D. *A Short History of Africa*. Baltimore, MD: Penguin, 1969.

Paden, W.D. *Tennyson in Egypt, A Study of the Imagery in His Earlier Work*. Lawrence, KS: University of Kansas, 1942.

Pope, Arthur Upham. *A Survey of Persian Art*. London: Oxford, 1939.

Pottinger, Henry. *Travels in Baloochistan and Sind*. London: 1816; Karachi: Indus, 1976.

Prussin, Labelle. "Architecture in Africa: An Annotated Bibliography," *Africana Library Journal*, 4:3 (1973), pp. 2-32.

_____. *The Architecture of Djenné: African Synthesis and Transformation*. Ann Arbor, MI: University Microfilms, 1974.

_____. "The Architecture of Islam in West Africa," *African Arts*, 1:2 (Winter 1968), pp. 32-35, 70-74.

_____. *Hatumere: Islamic Design in West Africa*. Berkeley: University of California Press, forthcoming.

_____. "An Introduction to Indigenous African Architecture," in *Journal of the Society of Architectural Historians*, 33:3 (October 1974), pp. 183-205.

_____. "Pillars, Projections, and Paradigms," in *Architectura*, 7:1 (1977), pp. 65-81.

_____. Review of René Gardi: *Indigenous African Architecture*, *African Arts*, 9:1 (October 1975), pp. 83-85.

_____. "Sudanese Architecture and the Manding," *African Arts* (Summer 1970), pp. 13-19, 64-67.

Rapoport, Amos. "An Approach to Vernacular Design," in James Marston Fitch, ed., *Shelter: Models of Native Ingenuity*. Katonah, NY: Katonah Gallery, 1982, pp. 43-48.

_____. "Cross-Cultural Aspects of Environmental Design," in *Environment and Culture*, Irwin Altman, Amos Rapoport, and Joachim F. Wohlwill, eds., *Human Behavior and Environment*, Vol. 4. New York: Plenum, 1980, pp. 7-46.

_____. *House Form and Culture*. Engelwood Cliffs, NJ: Prentice-Hall, 1969.

_____. "An Interview with Amos Rapoport on Vernacular Architecture," *M.E.T.U. Journal of the Faculty of Architecture*, 5:2 (Fall 1969), pp. 113-125.

Rapoport, Amos and Watson, Newton. "Cultural Variability in Physical Standards," in Robert Gutman, ed., *People and Buildings*. New York: Basic Books, 1972, pp. 33-53.

Ratcliff, Carter. "American Indian Masterworks," *Art International*, 18:2 (February 1974), pp. 28-29, 52.

Redfield, Robert. "Art and Icon," in Robert Redfield, et al, *Aspects of Primitive Art*. New York: Museum of Primitive Art, 1959, pp. 11-40.

Rudofsky, Bernard. *Architecture Without Architects*. New York: Museum of Modern Art, 1965.

_____. *The Prodigious Builders*. New York: Harcourt Brace Jovanovitch, 1977.

Rykwert, Joseph. *On Adam's House in Paradise*. Cambridge: Massachusetts Institute of Technology Press, 1981.

Safdie, Moshe. *Form and Purpose*. Boston: Houghton Mifflin, 1982.

Saint-Exupéry, Antoine de. *Terre des hommes* (1939). Gallimard, 1979.

_____. *Wind, Sand, and Stars*. London: Pan, 1979.

Schmertz, Mildred F. "Islamic Architecture and Rural Dwellings from Beijing to Kashi," *Architectural Record* (May 1982), pp. 92-101.

Schumacher, E.F. *Small is Beautiful*. New York: Harper and Row, 1975.

Shah, Mayank. "Nomadic Movements and Settlements of the Rabaris of Kutch," *Process Architecture*, 15 (1980) pp. 49-66.

Sontag, Susan. *On Photography*. New York: Delta, 1977.

Spencer, A.J. *Brick Architecture in Ancient Egypt*. Warminster, England: Aris and Phillips, 1979.

Stein, Richard. *Architecture and Energy*. Garden City, NY: Anchor, 1978.

Sun, Paul. "Underground Houses," *Mimar*, 3 (January-March 1982), pp. 42-47.

Timberlake, Lloyd. "Mud Can Make It," *Development Forum*, 9:7 (September 1981), p. 6.

Trilling, Lionel. *Sincerity and Authenticity*. Cambridge: Harvard University Press, 1972.

Vogel, Steven. "Organisms That Capture Currents," *Scientific American* (August 1978), pp. 128-139.

Watkin, David. *Morality and Architecture*. Oxford, Clarendon Press, 1977.

Wilde, Oscar. "The Critic as Artist," in Richard Ellmann, ed., *The Artist as Critic: Critical Writings of Oscar Wilde*. New York: Random House, 1969.

Wingert, Paul S. *Primitive Art: Its Traditions and Styles*. New York: Oxford, 1962.

Wright, John K. "Terrae Incognitae: The Place of the Imagination in Geography," in his *Human Nature in Geography*. Cambridge: Harvard University Press, 1966, pp. 68-88.

Wulff, Hans E. *The Traditional Crafts of Persia: Their Development, Technology, and Influence on Eastern and Western Civilizations*. Cambridge: Massachusetts Institute of Technology Press, 1966.

ACKNOWLEDGEMENTS

Is there life after library? James Ackerman warmly encouraged our belief that the open road may nourish the open mind. James Marston Fitch's enthusiasm and advice were extremely valuable.
We are grateful for the kindness and efficiency of the staff of Columbia University's superb Avery Architectural Library, particularly of Adolf Placzeck, Herbert Mitchell, and William O'Malley. At New York University's Bobst Library, we especially thank Arnold Markowitz.

The unknown is scary. For moral, material, and miscellaneous support toward lift-off, flight, and re-entry, our gratitude to Anna and Edward Reynolds, to Louise Bourgeois, and to Emily Allen, Randy Blom, Chan and Claire, Len Charlap, Ella Drucker, Sandie Ekhause, Barbara Giella, Penny Kirschenfeld, Jerry Maronek, Bernard H. Mendik, Dominique de Menil, Naomi Miller, Jane Owen, Nettie Tamler, and Sid Trommer.

In New York, Farouq Rishad's informed fervor profoundly stimulated our curiosity in his native Afghanistan. Once there, we were helped by many warm, proud people. We mourn the present political circumstances that force us to omit thanking any by name.
In India, the humanity and scrupulousness of Dilip Vaidya, Curator of the Kachchh Museum in Bhuj, were a great inspiration. In Kachchh, thanks to Gulberg, Habiban, Ali-Akbar, and Pupli Miya for their generous hospitality; to Dr. Rathore; and to the entire Harijan community of Janan. Thanks also to Carmel Berkson, Naueen Jaktau, Mahipat Javeradan, Jogi Krishna, Natawarllal Patel, the young

historian Durga Dan Ratnoo, and—for fine printing in Bombay of photos of people who befriended us on the road—to Razak A. Banatwala.

In Morocco, we particularly thank Baddi El Allaoui and Jean-Paul Ichter; in Mauritania, Mohammed el Heba ould Tfeil, the superb chef Ely ould Mohamed, Mohamedou ould Nefa, Sass ould Ba, and Koueiber ould N'Tcheh; in Mali, master mason of Djenné, Be Sao; in Niger, Dr. Gouro Abdulaye, Albert Ferral, and Michel Keita; in Senegal, Ibrahima Sall, Idrissa and Gaye.
For their votes of confidence in our work we thank James Ackerman, George Collins, Arthur Drexler, James Marston Fitch, Douglas Newton, Bernard Rudofsky, and Allen Wardwell.
For several fine translations of transparencies to black-and-white negatives, thanks to Gary Schneider.

For allowing us to mount the exhibition "Spectacular Vernacular," the basis of this book, at the Columbia Graduate School of Architecture and Planning, we thank Waltraude Schleicher-Woods, James Steward Polshek, and Arlene P. Jacobs. For subsequently arranging to host the show, we thank at Rutgers University, Thomas B. Shaw; at the Kling Partnership, Stevens and Elizabeth Sperling; at the Nassau County Hempstead Black History Museum, Phyllis Braff and Diana Hawkes; and at the Parsons School of Design's Gimbel Library, Christiane C. Collins. At the Smithsonian Institution Traveling Exhibition Services (SITES), which is now circulating the show, our deepest thanks go to Anne R. Gossett and to Lori Dempsey.

For subtlety and surgery during successive drafts, we are grateful to Buckley Jeppson and to Louanne Bulick, Mary Goldwater, Steven Kurtz, Eunice Lipton, Michael McTwigan, Larry Moss, Jay Schlesinger, Gibbs Smith, Tom Shaw, Dawn Stewart, and—as well as for the research and design of her excellent maps—Kate Thom.

Index

adobe, 8
Afghanistan, 2, 4, 6, 9, 12, 51-54, 68, 80-88
air-conditioning
    traditional, 53-68
    desert cooler, 68
    see wind devices
Algeria, 54
arabesques, 18-19
arcades, 42-49
architecture
    authenticity in, 14
    formal analysis of, 15
    glamour in, 90
    human touch in, 15, 91
    local symbols in, 15
    underground, 66
    see mud, adobe, vernacular architecture
architecture parlante, 88
Architecture Without Architects, 14
Arctic, as dry as desert, 5
artist, avant-garde, 14
authenticity, in architecture, 14
Bachelard, Gaston, 6
Bagdad, 69
Bambara, 69
Bamiyan, 2, 9, 80, 81, 87

beauty
    transcultural, 15
    of vernacular architecture, 15
Bodley, John, 89
brick, kiln baked, 5, 57, 69
Caillié, René, 3
caravan-ports, 3
cave, artificial, 5, 66
cement, 57, 90-91
Cervantes, 54
China, 4, 66
columns, 35, 42, 43, 50
construction materials
    modern, as alienating, 15
    see mud
consumerism, 57, 90, 91
cooling, evaporative, 68
    see ventilation
coursing, *see* mud
criticism
    impressive vs. expressive, 16
    architectural, 16
cultural geography, 15, 16
desert
    as moral landscape, 3
    image of, 1-4, 9, 11
    spatial experience of, 1
    variety of, 4
    see vernacular architecture

desert cooler, *see* air conditioning
development
    the term, 89
    vs. subsistence, 89
Djenné, 38, 39, 40
    house facade in, 29
    mosque in, 5, 70, 74, 75
domes
    Hausa, 50, 51
    ribless, 51
dust, 6, 62
ecology
    architecture rooted in, 91
    in traditional societies, 89
economies, market vs. traditional, 89
Egypt, 54, 68
energy
    cement's consumption of, 90-91
    high consumption of, 89
    rising cost of, 61
England, 90
    building with mud in, 5
fertility, symbols of, 18, 69, 72-73, 77, 85, 88
figure-ground effect, in decoration, 18, 42
formula, infant, 90
France, building with mud in, 5
Germany, building with mud in, 5
Harijan caste, 8, 22

Hausa dome, *see* domes
Hitchcock, Henry-Russell, 14
Hyderabad (Pakistan), 54-55, 58
igloo, 5
India, 4, 8, 22-25, 54, 68
industrialization, 14
   vs. vernacular values, 90
insulation, thermal, 5
   against ground damp, 5
Iran, 26, 53, 54, 62
Iraq, 18
Isfahan, 26
Islam, 69, 87, 88
Italy, 90
Kachchh, 22-25
Khoje Kheder, 87
La Mancha, 54
language, politics of, 89
Maadid, 62-67
machine, as cultural icon, 14
maintenance, 8, 10, 69
Mali, 5, 10, 16, 26-41, 43-46, 69-79
Mansa Musa, 69
materinity, symbols of, 18, 88
Matisse, Henri, 13
Mauritania, 3, 10, 17-21, 69
Mecca, 3, 69
Mexico, 4
mirrors, decorative, 22
missing-brick style, 27
Mohammed, 87
Mongolia, 54
Morocco, 3, 7, 12, 18, 62-67
mosque
   Sahelian, 5, 17, 69-79
   Afghan, 88
mud
   construction in, 7-8, 10-12, 13
   coursing, 8
   dependable, 6
   image of, 5

loss of building skills in, 90
pisé, 8
plaster, 8
rammed earth, 8
recipes, 8
shelters 1.5 billion, 4
stabilized, 90
thermal benefits, 5, 8
Muslim shrines, *see* ziarat
Neh, 54
Niger, 4, 13, 50
Niger River, 3
Nyerere, Julius, 91
ostrich eggs, 69-72, 77
Oualata, 3, 4, 69
Pakistan, 4, 54-61
Persian Gulf, 62
Peru, 68
phallic symbolism, 29, 38, 42, 69, 85, 88
photograph, limits knowledge of architecture, 15
Picasso, Pablo, 13
pigeon towers, 26
pisé, *see* mud
Pope, Alexander, 90
porches, 42
   free-standing, 54
primitive
   architecture, 13-14
   art, 13-14
   hut, 14
progress
   and infant formula, 90
   demythologized, 14
puddling, *see* mud
Quixote, Don, 54
Rabari caste, 22-25
rainy season, 4, 8, 10, 17-18, 69
rammed earth, *see* mud
roofs, 6, 8, 26-27, 50-51
Rudofsky, Bernard, 14
Sahel, 69-79

Saint-Exupery, Antoine de, 1
sandcastles, 5, 6
sculpture
   African, 13
   architecture as abstract, 54
   public, 15
Senegal, 42, 43, 47-49
shelter, vs. architecture, 14
Sind, 54-61
Sistan, 53-54
sky, desert vs. temperate, 6
snow
   as dry as sand, 5
   as building material, 5
solar collector, mud building as, 8
Solomon, 54
Sontag, Susan, 15
Southwest, United States, 4, 8, 68
Spain, 8, 54, 66
stack effect, 62-67
stepped-recession style, 27
subsistence, 89
Tanzania, 91
Tatta, 56-61
technology
   appropriate, 91
   demythologized, 14
   vs. tradition, 15
temperate climate
   building in mud in, 5
   function of architecture in, 6
Tennyson, Alfred Lord, 3
thermal benefit
   cement's poor, 91
   of high relief, 27, 42
Tibet, 54
Timbuctoo
   as myth, 3
   Tennyson on, 3
toilet, 39, 58, 65
Trilling, Lionel, 14

tropics, architecture in humid vs. dry, 6
Tunisia, 66
Turkey, 66
Untouchables, *see* Harijan
vault, 51
Venice, 90
ventilation, 6, 54-68
ventilators, 54, 56
vernacular
 etymology of, 91
 values, 91
vernacular architecture
 and photography, 15
 as touchtone of purity, 14
 defined, ix., 98, *fn.* 24
 in humid vs. dry tropics, 6
 perceived as vital, 90
 perceived as doomed, 90
 term first used, 91
 term misapplied, 70
 see vernacular
voluntary simplicity, 91
walls, 17-49
 embossed, 22-25
 in humid vs. dry tropics, 6
 painted and incised, 16-21
 undecorated, 17
 with high relief, 26-41
 see arcades, columns
water
 and architectural site, 5
 cement's use of, 90-91
 evaporative cooling, 68
waterfall, 5
Wilde, Oscar, 16
wind
 desert, 53-62
 devices, 53-62, 68
 shadow, 54
wind-catchers, 54-61
 made of concrete, 61

windmills, 53-54
windows, absence friendly in desert, 6, 7, 66, 68
windscoops, 54
women
 Afghan, 88
 breast feeding vs. formula, 90
 decorate buildings, 8, 16-21
 maintain buildings, 7
Yahya El Kamel, 69
Young Men's House, 29, 37, 42
ziarat, 80-88

Art historian and critic Jean-Louis Bourgeois is a graduate of Harvard, where he won the James Bowdoin Prize. Photographer Carollee Pelos has had several solo exhibitions. Their articles on earth architecture have appeared in *Natural History, Architectural Review, Architectural Design, Mimar,* and *Soft Energy Notes.* Circulated by the Smithsonian, their exhibition, also called "Spectacular Vernacular," is touring nationally and abroad. Manhattan-based Pelos and Bourgeois lecture widely. They are suckers for cats, flea markets, and old postcards.